True Crime Stories of the LOWCOUNTRY

True Crime Stories of the LOWCOUNTRY

CATHY PICKENS

THE History PRESS

Published by The History Press
An imprint of Arcadia Publishing
Charleston, SC
www.historypress.com

Front cover, top: St. Philip's gravestones. *Jim Sill on flickr.com*; *bottom*: Al Capone. Chicago *Beaureau (Federal Bureau of Investigation) on Wikimedia Commons. Back cover, top*: Myrtle Beach high-rises. *Gene Gallin on Unsplash*; *bottom*: Charleston County Courthouse. *Historic American Buildings Survey—National Parks Service on Wikimedia Commons.*

First published 2025

Manufactured in the United States

ISBN 9781467158961

Library of Congress Control Number: 2026941145

Notice: The information in this book is true and complete to the best of our knowledge. It is offered without guarantee on the part of the author or The History Press. The author and The History Press disclaim all liability in connection with the use of this book.

To the reporters and photographers who have recorded South Carolina history and the librarians and archivists who make it available so we don't lose it and don't forget. Thanks for the stories.

CONTENTS

ACKNOWLEDGEMENTS

Elizabeth, Tom and Larry, for their expert advice and sharp-eyed reading of early drafts of this book. (All mistakes, of course, remain mine.)

Sherrill Shiraz, the generous and wizardly research expert at Everett Library, Queens University of Charlotte.

Loyd Dillon, artist, teacher, amazingly funny and kind person, whose sketches are a delight.

Keith Vincent and his remarkable collection of postcards showing courthouses around the United States and throughout history. See Courthousehistory.com.

Chad Rhoad, Jonny Foster, Abigail Fleming and the rest of the talented team at The History Press.

WELCOME

Lowcountry South Carolina is marked by variety and contrast. To some, the region sparks images of sandy beaches, with family gatherings and teenage frolics at Myrtle Beach and the Grand Strand. To others, it conjures pictures of stately eighteenth- and nineteenth-century mansions, cobblestoned streets and horse-drawn carriages in Charleston or Beaufort or the attraction of golf courses dotting the sweep of the coast, culminating in the Harbour Town course on exclusive Hilton Head, site of the annual Heritage golf tournament. None of these highlights along the coast are the full story of the Lowcountry unless you also know the swamps and piney woods, the ancient live oaks draped in Spanish moss, the rich, dark earth that fed families and created wealth for the region for centuries and the small towns where residents have known each other for generations.

The English, Spanish and French tried to establish outposts on the coast as early as the mid-1500s. In 1670, the English founded the first permanent settlement in what became known as Charles Town to honor King Charles II. Eventually, settlers moved inland seeking more land to farm. Contrary to the South portrayed in *Gone with the Wind*, cotton wasn't the state's first or the richest cash crop. Rice dominated the colonial economy and built fortunes. Extensive fields were flooded and drained with elaborate mechanical means constructed by the backbreaking work and craftsmanship of Africans and Caribbean islanders who understood tidal plains agriculture. Remnants of those rice fields works can still be found inland along the creeks and canals. In the mid-1700s, thanks to the creative efforts of entrepreneur Eliza Lucas

The Angel Oak on Johns Island, one of the nation's largest and oldest live oak trees (age estimated at four to five hundred years), predates the state's oldest European settlers. *Photo by Jim Molloy on Unsplash.*

Pinckney, indigo cultivation and export became the second most lucrative crop. Cotton became important by 1800, after the cotton gin was invented, but within a few decades, the boll weevil—dubbed a "wave of evil"—devastated cotton production and caused many farmers to move inland from the region.

Early settlers in the coastal region battled heat and humidity, smallpox outbreaks, mosquitos bearing dreaded yellow fever and malaria, deadly snakes, tropical storms and devastating hurricanes. One colonial proverb warned, "They who want to die quickly, go to Carolina." The region wasn't always an easy place to live.

How, exactly, to draw boundaries around such a diverse region? From early days, the state was divided into two sections, as summed up in a 1986 U.S. Geological Survey centenary review:

> *Because the Up Country and the Low Country differed in customs, economy, and history, a strong strain of sectionalism existed (and some would say still exists) in South Carolina. The Low Country was dominated by the cultural and economic influence of Charleston, a city that had been long established by the 1880's. The Up Country had no one dominant center, and it was decidedly rural, even still partially unsettled in the 1800's.*

In the broadest definition, the "Lowcountry" is the lower half of the state, from the coast to the Midlands' sandhills that stretch on either side of Columbia. Some, though, define the Lowcountry only as the counties around and south of Charleston. At first glance, the beaches, the inland farms and the historic cities of Charleston and Beaufort aren't similar enough to seem related. But the close historic links between the tidewater regions and the farms along the inland blackwater rivers make the region—and its crime stories—difficult to separate, so we'll explore the entire Lowcountry region.

With its diversity, the Lowcountry offers plenty of unusual crime stories, all of which reveal and shape the uniqueness of the coastal region of South Carolina. Vacation spots often attract roaming serial killers or those bent on a crime spree, as well as teenagers wanting to cut loose and have a good time who flock to Myrtle Beach. In a long-settled region, families build dynasties; some abuse their power, to the point of getting away with murder. Stir in bootleggers in a place called Hell Hole Swamp, more than one offbeat law enforcer, an enslaved man who was freed by

The pyramid mausoleum is one of many unique tombs in Charleston's Magnolia Cemetery. *Courtesy of Michelle via Unsplash.*

Horse carriage tour on Charleston's Broad Street traveling toward St. Michael's Church. *Courtesy of Srini Somanchi via Unsplash.*

his poison cure and a Lizard Man, and you've got a start on the stories that have helped make Lowcountry South Carolina a colorful, intriguing Southern gem.

My family has been in the Carolinas for more than three hundred years. Because any telling naturally depends on the storyteller's choices, these are cases that, for one reason and another, captured my imagination. My first book for The History Press was *Charleston Mysteries*, a walking tour of mysteries and ghost stories; I've included expanded versions of crimes in a couple of those tales. I'm excited to explore more of this rich, colorful region.

This book is not a work of investigative journalism. The information is drawn solely from published or broadcast resources—newspapers, television documentaries, podcasts, books, scholarly papers, print and online articles. One of the drawbacks in recounting historical events is that accounts vary. Some reported "facts" aren't accurate, or they're at odds with someone else's memory or perception of the event. While I have worked to dig out as many points of view as I could find, I'm sure there are mistakes. My apologies in advance.

For me, what fascinates is not random violence but rather people, their lives and their relationships. Some of these stories could have happened anywhere. Some made huge headlines far away from South Carolina.

Others remain writ large mostly in the hearts of the family and friends of those involved.

The stories, woven together, demonstrate the rich variety of those who call this part of the state home. These are stories that have helped shape South Carolina's Lowcountry. People and their pasts matter here. The stories are worth remembering, even when they involve loss and especially when they are tempered with affection and deep memories.

The epigraph for the 1872 *The Newspaper Press*, a history of early Charleston by William L. King, summed up the importance of remembering:

Well did our papers here display the times;
Some streak'd with follies; others, stain'd with crimes.

Welcome to coastal South Carolina and its crime stories.

Map of Lowcountry crime locations. *Courtesy of Cathy Pickens.*

1
THE POISONERS

The Black Widow

In September 1975, John Van Bazen sat on the witness stand in the Florence County Courthouse and testified about his harrowing experience a year earlier. He and his wife had moved in with her mother, Emily Stone Conyers, in the summer of 1974. Two months later, he was rushed to the hospital in Florence, nauseated and weak. A few weeks after that hospital visit, he went to the Veterans Administration Hospital in Charleston complaining of even more extreme symptoms: back pain, increasingly blurry vision and loss of the use of his hands and legs. The VA doctors soon diagnosed arsenic poisoning; his hair samples showed a level fifty times higher than the normal amount found in a human body.

The VA staff notified local law enforcement, launching a five-month investigation uncovering other suspicious activity in the family. Too many people related to Emily Conyers, a fifty-three-year-old widow and mother of four, had died unexpectedly. Exhumations of three bodies in three different county cemeteries gathered evidence that Emily had poisoned her two husbands—Willie Graham Stone (age fifty-two) in 1967 and Milton Reece Conyers (age thirty-seven) in 1973. She also unsuccessfully tried to kill her mother-in-law (who died of lung cancer in 1972; elevated arsenic levels were found in her hair when her body was exhumed). The targets who survived included her son-in-law John Van Bazen and Iris Stevens, her

The renovated façade of High School of Charleston, built in 1921, which became part of the Medical University of South Carolina (MUSC). *Courtesy of Warren LeMay via Flickr.*

second husband's cousin. Cousin Iris testified that Emily poisoned her when she refused to let Emily buy an interest in her flower shop. Emily and Milton were already business owners in Pamplico, operating a fabric shop, and Emily apparently wanted to expand her business holdings.

Initially, the county solicitor—as South Carolina calls its district attorneys or prosecutors—charged her in the death of her second husband but brought no charges for her other supposed victims. At trial, Medical University of South Carolina professor Dr. Richard H. Gadsden served as an expert witness for the prosecution. Milton Conyers died two years before the trial, but arsenic is a heavy metal and doesn't disappear; the post-exhumation autopsy revealed as much as one hundred times the expected amount of arsenic. For the jury, solicitor Kenneth Summerford recapped the professor's evidence: "In other words, this man was loaded with arsenic?" The professor replied, "That's one way to put it."

Proving a poisoning case can be challenging: Did the defendant have access to the poison? How was it administered? Do the opportunities to administer poison coincide with the victim's symptoms? The trial testimony about the levels of arsenic found in the bodies got a bit tedious. The courtroom had been packed all week with onlookers, many of them women from Pamplico interested in the proceedings. But on Thursday, during the technical testimony about grains versus milligrams of arsenic, the news reporter noted that "the standing room only crowd thinned leaving several vacant seats and some spectators dozed." At one point, the judge said, "I'm glad I studied law instead of this."

While jurors must learn about how much poison it takes to kill, how much was found and how it got inside the victim, prosecutors don't have to prove motive. But motive is an element that jurors are always curious to understand. As is often the case with domestic poisoning cases, the heinous, excruciating murder method seemed out of proportion with the hoped-for gain. From Milton Conyers's death, Emily collected $5,000 in life insurance (over $35,000 today). She'd clearly hoped for more: he had two policies, one for $1,000 and one for $10,000, but the company determined that her husband was an alcoholic with suicidal tendencies and they therefore reduced her payout.

But what were the motives for the other victims? Emily's daughter and son-in-law John had been living with her for a couple of months during a period of some marital upheaval. His illness started about the time the couple appeared to be reconciling. With her husband's cousin Iris, Emily seemed irritated by Iris's refusal to let her buy into her business. And her mother-in-law? She had cancer, so why poison her? What seemed inconsequential to others must have been important to Emily.

The closing arguments at the end of the testimony were, at times, hard-fought and heated. Solicitor T. Kenneth Summerford painted Emily Conyers as a woman who thought she could kill with impunity, collect insurance or inherit property and move on to another victim. "She almost got by with it," he said, "except for one little accident—John Van Bazen. He didn't die." Emily's defense attorney, Richard Dusenbury, argued that all five victims together had less than "one three hundredths of a teaspoon" of arsenic in them. Solicitor Summerford called that a "bunch of mathematical hogwash." They also disputed how much money she collected after Mr. Conyers's death. The newspaper reported that Summerford shouted, "It's not the amount you receive, it's the amount you think you're gonna get."

On October 3, 1975, at the end of a weeklong trial and after deliberating only one hour, the jury returned at 5:30 p.m. and found Emily Conyers guilty of the poisoning murder of Milton Conyers. Some of Emily's criminal actions occurred before a 1972 decision by the U.S. Supreme Court that temporarily suspended the death penalty, ruling its application was arbitrary and capricious. By 1974, South Carolina had rewritten its law and reinstated the death penalty option, but because Milton's 1973 murder occurred during the moratorium, she was not eligible for the death penalty.

In March 1977, an appeal to the state supreme court granted Emily Conyers a new trial for Milton's death. The court held that it was proper for the trial judge to allow evidence about the poisoning of the three victims who survived but ruled it an error to admit evidence about the poisoning of her first husband, Willie Graham Stone, who died six years before Conyers's death. Stone's autopsy revealed the highest measured arsenic levels in any of her supposed victims (between one hundred and one thousand times a normal level of arsenic, according to different experts), but the appellate court held that the only evidence connecting her to his death was "that she

The old Florence County Courthouse, located at 181 Irby Street in Florence, was built in 1972. *Courtesy of Carol M. Highsmith Archive, Library of Congress, Prints and Photographs Division.*

was his wife and he had some life insurance." The prosecution presented nothing to establish how or when she delivered the poison.

In May 1977, Emily and her lawyers were back in a Florence courtroom—not for a retrial of her husband's murder but for the poisoning of her son-in-law. The news account of the hearing reported that she "clutched a small purse and a black handbag was slung across her shoulder," a focus on fashion detail rarely if ever reported about male defendants.

Before the judge, she pleaded guilty to assault with intent to kill in the poisoning of John Van Bazen. His illness and diagnosis at the VA Hospital in Charleston was what initially led law enforcement to the other victims. John was able to testify that he became ill after eating meals that she prepared, which was the element missing in the case of Emily's first husband. She accepted a fifteen-year sentence for John's poisoning. Given time served, she would be eligible for parole in about three years.

She'd also been charged in the poison deaths of two husbands and for administering poison to two other victims, but as part of the plea deal, the solicitor placed those other charges "on the contingent docket"—which meant they weren't dropped but they wouldn't be pursued unless circumstances merited prosecution. As with their previous exchanges, her defense attorney presented a slightly different slant on the outcome: that all the other charges had been "cleared up and will not be held against her." In any event, Emily Conyers disappeared into the state prison system for a few years and didn't make headlines again.

Poison and Punitive Damages

Punitive or "exemplary" damages are awarded in civil—not criminal—cases and are designed to punish the defendant for willful, wanton or reckless behavior. The money is awarded because the defendant's conduct was so extreme, it deserves to be punished or made an example for others.

The nation's first punitive damages award was granted in a South Carolina court in 1784, lagging England's first punitive award by only twenty-one years. The community of Jacksonborough (today called Jacksonboro), located between Charleston and Beaufort near the Edisto River, was the scene of some hardcore partying with a local physician named Norris, a "foreigner" named Genay and others. According to the court report, an argument between the doctor and the outsider grew so heated that "to adjust this quarrel, pistols were introduced." According to the well-worn rules of dueling, seconds were appointed for the duelers and "powder was fired off at each other," resulting in a "pretended reconciliation." Glasses of wine were poured to smooth tensions. As a final secret jab at his opponent, Dr. Norris managed to slip a large quantity of cantharides or "Spanish fly" into Genay's conciliatory drink.

Genay, the "only person who thought the altercation serious," quaffed his wine and left for his home. Before long, the poison took effect. He summoned a Dr. Wallace, who found his patient in "extreme and excruciating pain," which lasted almost two weeks.

Spanish fly is made from crushing one of the many varieties of blister beetles to obtain the cantharidin secretions. It causes skin blistering, and its most common medical use was to burn off warts. In folk medicine and pop culture, though, Spanish fly is an aphrodisiac—with dangerous and deadly side effects. In a well-known cautionary tale from 1954, a married London office manager at a chemical company let his daydreams about his lovely coworker Betty Grant override his good sense. Manager Arthur Ford was no chemist, but he understood that a little cantharidin might cause Miss Grant to find his blandishments irresistible. He snuck enough from the chemical storeroom to kill two hundred people, doctored a couple of chocolate-covered coconut squares in the bag of treats he brought back after lunch and purposefully handed one to Grant and one to another woman—with a bit for himself.

While cantharidin can cause inflammation and irritation, which led to its rumored love-potion powers, too much can result in a high heart rate, gastrointestinal and urinary distress, hemorrhage and even death. The three office workers were rushed to the hospital. The two women each ate about ten times a lethal dose and did not survive their after-lunch coconut candies. Arthur Ford, who ate a small dose and survived, pleaded guilty to manslaughter and was sentenced to five years. A news account reported that his wife had forgiven him.

Almost two hundred years before Arthur Ford's trial, at the Colleton County trial for Genay's poisoning, Dr. Norris's counsel maintained that he accidentally administered more than he intended and certainly meant no harm. It was nothing more than a drunken frolic, just as Arthur Ford later saw no harm in his ill-fated London lovemaking attempt.

The South Carolina judge didn't think much of the "frolic" defense, finding it a "very wanton outrage upon a stranger in the country" by a medical man who couldn't pretend he didn't know how powerful the potion

The community of Jacksonboro is located on Highway 17 near the Edisto River, between Charleston and Beaufort. *Courtesy of LittleT889 via Wikimedia Commons.*

was. Since this was a civil case rather than a criminal one, the judge awarded the injured Genay "very exemplary damages" for his pain and suffering in the amount of about $25,000 in today's dollars.

THE POISON CURE

In 1749, with an unprecedented invitation, a man known as Dr. Caesar appeared before a committee of the South Carolina Commons House of Assembly to report on his poison cure. Dr. Caesar's reputation as a healer had spread among the plantations outside Charleston, particularly in what are now Colleton and Dorchester Counties. The legislative committee had interviewed four white plantation owners respected in the community, and all touted the success of the doctor's cures for rattlesnake bites and for mysterious poisonings. One who testified of his own personal cure was Henry Middleton, who later served as a president of the nation's Continental Congress.

As reported by Nick Butler and the *Charleston Time Machine* project at the Charleston County Public Library, little is known about Dr. Caesar other than that he was Black, enslaved and sixty-seven years old—"nearly as old as the colony of South Carolina." Nothing else was recorded about his appearance or background, according to Butler, "so we don't know whether Caesar was a native of Africa or had been born in South Carolina" or whether he spoke English or Gullah. But his enslaver, a militia captain named John Norman, said he'd "never known him to fail in any one attempt" at treating a patient. Other plantation owners in the region knew of Caesar's gifts—and were willing to testify before the state assembly in his support.

Those living in the often-brutal climate of coastal South Carolina faced snakes, bugs, parasites, plant irritants and myriad little-understood diseases and were armed with limited medical knowledge. They were willing to ask for Dr. Caesar's help and willing to pay for his knowledge.

His price? He told them that "he expected his freedom, and a moderate competence for life, which he hoped the committee would be of opinion deserved one hundred pounds currency per annum. And he proposed to give the committee any satisfactory experiment of his ability they please, as soon as he should be able to provide himself with the necessary ingredients." The assembly met his request and went a step further, offering him additional payments if he made any future discoveries that might benefit the citizens. They also paid John Norman £500 for the freedom of Dr. Caesar, provided the concoctions were proven to work by the testimony of leading citizens who'd been cured when treatments by the region's top medical men had failed.

In March 1750, the report to the assembly announced that the cures worked. As agreed, Dr. Caesar made public his recipes and his treatment procedures. "Plantane and wild Hoare-hound," roots and branches gathered in the summer, were the principal ingredients in his poison cure. Dr. Caesar also used goldenrod, sassafras and wood ash and used a "leaf of good tobacco moistened with rum" as a poultice to hold the cure on a rattlesnake wound.

The *South Carolina Gazette*, the first regularly published newspaper in the state, printed the recipes for his cures, which soon spread to the other American colonies and to Great Britain.

Correctly diagnosing a poisoning can be difficult, even with modern medical testing. Imagine the challenges in the mid-eighteenth century of separating malicious poisoning from natural illnesses, much less treating or curing any of those. In 2015, historian Dr. Claire Gherini published an evaluation of Dr. Caesar's work. She pointed out that the state's assembly, in

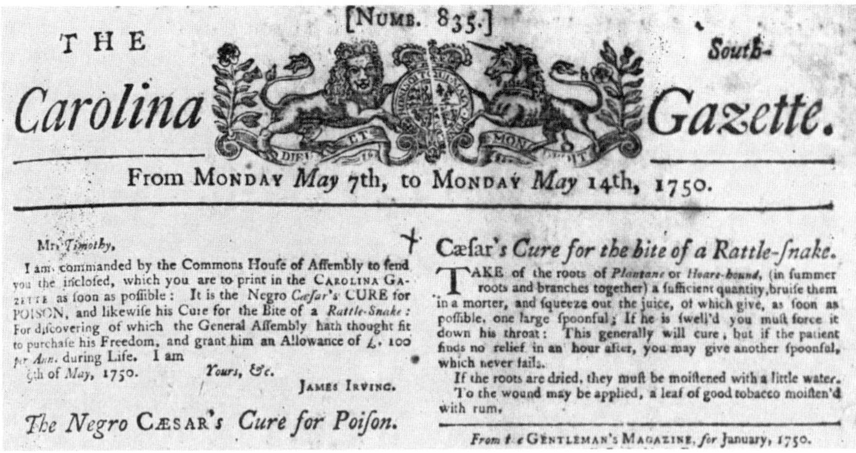

[NUMB. 835.]

THE South-Carolina Gazette.

From MONDAY *May* 7th, to MONDAY *May* 14th, 1750.

Mr. *Timothy*,

I am commanded by the Commons House of Assembly to send you the inclosed, which you are to print in the CAROLINA GAZETTE as soon as possible: It is the Negro *Cæsar's* CURE for POISON, and likewise his Cure for the Bite of a *Rattle-Snake*: For discovering of which the General Assembly hath thought fit to purchase his Freedom, and grant him an Allowance of £. 100 *per Ann.* during Life. I am

9th of *May*, 1750.

Yours, &c.

JAMES IRVING.

The Negro CÆSAR's *Cure for Poison.*

Cæsar's *Cure for the bite of a Rattle-snake.*

TAKE of the roots of *Plantane* or *Hoare-hound*, (in summer roots and branches together) a sufficient quantity, bruise them in a morter, and squeeze out the juice, of which give, as soon as possible, one large spoonful; If he is swell'd you must force it down his throat: This generally will cure, but if the patient finds no relief in an hour after, you may give another spoonful, which never fails.

If the roots are dried, they must be moistened with a little water.

To the wound may be applied, a leaf of good tobacco moisten'd with rum.

From the GENTLEMAN'S MAGAZINE, *for* January, 1750.

The news about Dr. Caesar's cure was first published on the front page of *The Carolina Gazette* in Charleston, May 7, 1750. *Courtesy of* The Carolina Gazette *via newspapers.com.*

assessing his work, focused on his ability as a diagnostician. However, they could have chosen a more scientific method, such as animal testing—which had been used in the colony twenty years earlier to see if antimony could be used as an antidote for snakebite. Dr. Gherini also pointed out they could have referred to books on plants and their properties. As it turns out, both horehound and broadleaf plantain (also called rattlesnake plant) had long been used in many cultures for treating snakebite and other poisoning.

They chose, though, to believe in Dr. Caesar. For the assembly members, testimony by a few good men that the cure worked was sufficient without messy experiments and tests. Dr. Caesar was freed, his stipend paid and his famous recipes widely shared.

2
LOVE GONE WRONG

Where There's a Will...or a Life Insurance Policy

"If anything happens to me, be sure and look at (husband, wife, significant other)." Or even more directly: "I think he's trying to kill me." Those prophetic statements by a spouse or significant other are chilling, especially against a backdrop of domestic violence—or a sudden death. In the early 2000s, Teresa Hanna told more than one person on more than one occasion that she was afraid her husband, Davy, was trying to kill her. Not that he *might*, said Teresa, who served as the assistant Johnsonville city administrator, but that she thought he'd already tried. The time she'd fallen out of their boat on the Intracoastal Waterway near Georgetown, she told friends she didn't think he would've pulled her out of the water if another boat hadn't been close enough to see what was happening. He'd told her that "if he ever wanted to get rid of her, all it would take was a six pack of beer," presumably to bribe someone to do it for him.

During their ten-year marriage, Teresa and Davy Hanna had experienced "serious discord," as the appellate court termed it. Her dire prophecies apparently came true early on August 15, 2003. Teresa's father-in-law, Ronnie Hanna, found her lying in her driveway, fatally shot five times with a .22-caliber rifle. Paramedics arrived, followed by SLED (South Carolina Law Enforcement Division) investigators. Davy came home and began telling investigators they needed to look at Teresa's boss, not at him.

While pointing to another suspect, Davy also quickly contacted insurance companies concerning several policies on Teresa's life worth $276,000. In September, credit insurance paid the loan on Davy's truck. Davy kept checking with other companies to learn the status of their expected payouts—until October 30, when he and his brother Darry were arrested and charged with Teresa's murder.

Both were sitting in the county jail, and rules wouldn't allow the brothers, as prisoners, to communicate directly with each other by phone or in person. On November 22, Davy used the jail phone system—on which users are reminded that calls are always recorded—to let Darry's girlfriend know he was sending Darry a letter secreted in a box of soap. Naturally, a jail officer intercepted the soapbox and the handwritten letter inside, which bore the heading "Our Way Out." The letter explained Davy's plan for both brothers to die by suicide after they wrote letters pinning the murder on Teresa's boss.

That brilliant plan was foiled. The two were set to stand trial in August 2005, two years after Teresa's murder. The prosecution in a criminal trial, which has the burden of proving that the defendant committed a crime, presented its case first. At the close of the state's evidence, defense counsel made a motion for a directed verdict, arguing the state failed to present sufficient evidence for the jury to convict of a crime. The judge surprised the courtroom by agreeing and issued a directed verdict acquitting the brothers—a rare outcome in a criminal case.

The brothers were free, and the state prosecutor could not appeal the decision or try them again for the murder.

Despite the defeat in state court, Florence County prosecutor Ed Clements III felt strongly that the case against the Hanna brothers had merit. As a last resort, he approached federal prosecutors about bringing federal charges against the brothers. Under the U.S. Constitution, double jeopardy protects citizens from being tried twice for the same crime; it doesn't protect from being tried for a different crime. A new trial can be based on the same facts as long as the crime charged is different.

A year later, the brothers were indicted in federal court—not for the state charge of murder but for twenty-two federal counts, including mail and wire fraud. The heart of the federal charges was the brothers' conspiracy and their use of the U.S. Postal Service and electronic communications with intent to commit fraud and collect on Teresa's insurance.

Teresa's murder prompted both prosecutions, but the state homicide statute and the federal fraud and conspiracy statutes delineate different crimes.

The federal indictments were dated August 9, 2006. The brothers were held in the Florence County Detention Center in Effingham pending their trip to federal court. On August 26, Davy used a bedsheet and hanged himself from a sprinkler head in his cell.

Meanwhile, Darry was talking to some of his fellow inmates, explaining how he'd helped his brother in exchange for 30 percent of the insurance money. He also complained that his older brother hadn't bothered writing a letter before he killed himself, taking full responsibility and letting Darry off the hook. Thanks to his brother's lack of consideration, there he sat in jail, awaiting trial. The inmates shared Darry's admissions with investigators.

In February 2007, Darry's trial in the federal courthouse in Florence—about two blocks from the county courthouse where he'd been acquitted of the state murder charge—ended with his conviction on all twenty-two counts. He was in his mid-twenties and sentenced to 440 years in federal prison—the maximum sentence of 20 years for each offense.

On appeal, the defense asked the Fourth Circuit Court of Appeals to set aside Darry's conviction because the judge shouldn't have admitted the letter Darry wrote to his brother while in prison or the statements made by Teresa before her death about his threats.

Typically, statements from a victim would be admitted only if the killing took place to keep the victim from speaking. On a fine point of law, Darry hadn't *intended* to silence Teresa to keep her from talking; instead, he'd killed her to collect her insurance. Darry's goal was her insurance money, not to keep her from testifying against him or Davy, so her statements couldn't be admitted under that hearsay exception.

However, the court ruled that many of her statements were admissible under the state-of-mind exception to the hearsay rule, so admitting the challenged statements did not prejudice Darry's case and weren't grounds for overturning the conviction. The court said the prosecution introduced plenty of other evidence that established Davy's motive to collect insurance and about his suspicious conduct, including his infidelity, his lies about marital problems and about having no life insurance on Teresa, his failure to mention owning more than one .22 rifle and his suicide. Given the accumulation of evidence, the admission of her statements was harmless.

In addition, Davy's "Our Way Out" letter was admissible to show his state of mind. Arguments before the trial judge about admitting the letter filled almost 150 pages of the trial transcript, so the issue had been thoroughly vetted by the judge and the lawyers. In addition, any issues with the letter were made harmless by Darry's own admissions to other inmates.

The appellate court upheld Darry's conviction.

Fifteen years later, in April 2022, forty-three-year-old Darry Hanna was serving his sentence in a medium-security federal prison in northern West Virginia. He filed a *pro se* (filed on his own behalf) motion seeking a sentence reduction under the federal compassionate release statute. He outlined the self-improvement courses he'd taken, but he did not present evidence of poor health or other reason why he deserved compassionate release, other than that his sentence "is longer than necessary…to achieve the goals of sentencing."

The court found that, even though he had no lengthy criminal history, the circumstance of the murder "outweighs his law-abiding past." With premeditation, he shot his sister-in-law five times with a high-power rifle, first in the face, while standing one to five feet from her, for the planned purpose of sharing in her life insurance. The appellate court again upheld his sentence. As a rule, federal prisoners sentenced after 1987 serve their full sentences. He is scheduled for release on May 24, 2380.

Deadly Charleston Love Triangle

True in the twenty-first century and certainly true in Victorian-era 1889 Charleston, sex scandals always make for good gossip—and sometimes they make banner news headlines.

The city was still repairing itself, economically, physically and socially, from the ravages of the Civil War. In April 1861, the first shot had been fired from the Battery in Charleston toward Federal troops holding Fort Sumter, sitting guard at the mouth of Charleston Harbor. The locals anticipated a simple skirmish and that the fighting would soon be finished. The next four bloody, destructive years would leave only remnants of that self-assured society.

In the war's aftermath, Confederate Captain Francis Warrington Dawson became one of the city's stalwart leaders. In 1886, a massive earthquake—the strongest quake to ever hit the eastern United States—crumbled the city. The tremors were felt as far away as Chicago and New York City. An estimated two thousand buildings were damaged and sixty people died.

As editor of the *Charleston News and Courier*, Dawson made certain that his presses were running, that his papers were distributed the next day and word got out to the wire services. The earthquake's aftershocks continued to keep the citizenry on edge, and they needed to be reassured that something in their world was operating as it should. They needed information, and those outside the city had to be alerted that help was required.

Photographs and reports of Hibernian Hall's broken columns littering Meeting Street, the damage to St. Michael's Church and other public buildings, cracked and broken businesses and residences were widely reported thanks to Dawson's work. People lived in the parks and streets because their houses were uninhabitable or because of fear of the continuing smaller quakes. Supply routes bringing food, medical supplies and other relief were disrupted. Throughout the recovery, Dawson and his newspaper were engaged in the civic business of healing the city.

Even businesslike and determined public figures like Captain Dawson also have private lives and families that need their guidance, protection and leadership. On the afternoon of March 12, 1889, the imposing Captain Dawson strode down the street, cane in hand. He faced an unpleasant but necessary task, settling a personal matter with Dr. Thomas McDow.

Dr. McDow was a newcomer to Charleston, not always an easy place to settle among the families who'd called the city home for generations. He and his wealthy German wife had come to set up his medical practice at 101 Rutledge Street, only blocks from the present-day locations of Roper Hospital and the Medical University of South Carolina (MUSC). The McDow house was a short walk around the corner from the Dawsons' house at 99 Bull Street.

In 2011, authors Susan Millar Williams and Stephen G. Hoffius detailed in their book *Upheaval in Charleston* the story of the earthquake and the later contentiousness between Captain Dawson and Dr. McDow. Dr. McDow

Opposite: The most damaging earthquake in the southeastern United States struck Charleston in 1886, damaging almost every structure in the city. *Courtesy of University of South Carolina via Wikimedia Commons.*

Above: The home and office of Dr. Thomas McDow at 101 Rutledge Avenue in Charleston. *Courtesy of Historic American Buildings Survey, Library of Congress.*

met petite, attractive twenty-two-year-old Hélène Burdayron when she came to the doctor's office to request a house call. The Dawsons' cook had a sick baby. Hélène worked for the Dawson family helping with the children—though some said she was more of a visitor and friend of the captain's wife, Sarah, than hired help.

From that first meeting, Dr. McDow quickly became obsessed with the governess; his behavior would today be called stalking. He lingered on the sidewalk, watching for her to pass in a carriage or on foot. He stopped her on the street to talk. He brought her bouquets of flowers. He quickly proposed marriage, saying he'd go to North Carolina to file for divorce from the wife he'd married only for her money. South Carolina rigidly opposed divorce; except for a short period during Reconstruction, divorce wasn't legal in the state until 1949.

At first, Hélène rebuffed the doctor's overtures, thinking he must be drunk or mad. But soon enough, she was spending time with him in the garden and, when the Dawsons were out of town, entertaining him behind the closed doors of the family's library. He gave her a gold watch. She loaned him one of the Dawsons' books, the novel *'Twixt Love and Law*, the story of a single girl's love for a married man.

Later summaries of the case often omit interesting details provided by Williams and Hoffius. Captain Dawson's house servants had told him that Hélène was keeping improper company. He confronted her, and she, certain of his wife Sarah's friendship, defied him. What she did was none of his business. Captain Dawson asked the chief of police, as a personal favor, to have Hélène surveilled. The report did Hélène no credit—she was regularly seeing the married Dr. McDow. What's more, McDow had another young lover tucked away in a house nearby. And he was under investigation for aiding a life insurance scam by providing fake death certificates. The police chief warned Captain Dawson not to confront Dr. McDow. With his world closing in around him, the doctor could be dangerous. Dawson chose to ignore the police chief's warning.

On March 12, after finishing some editorial work in his newspaper office, Captain Dawson took the horse trolley to Rutledge Street. Rather than turning toward his house, he walked around the corner and called at McDow's ground-floor office.

Standing together in his medical examining room, McDow surely felt outmatched. Dawson was a well-regarded military captain with a domineering physical presence. And he was angry, punctuating his demands with the cane in his hand. McDow was short and slightly built. Later, McDow said that

Dawson began beating him with that cane, and the situation became so threatening that he was left with no choice. He pulled his pistol and fired.

When a gunshot rang out, McDow's wife, her afternoon visitor (who incidentally was McDow's secret lover) and the house servants could not help but hear it. A passing coachman and a peanut-cake seller heard something and raised the alarm. When a patrolling police officer knocked on McDow's door, the doctor opened it only a crack, said all was fine and sent him on his way.

Inside, McDow noted that Dawson wasn't visibly bleeding, but his medical training told him the bullet had done its damage internally. His reaction looked like an inept comedy skit, except the circumstances were real and tragic. Confused, frightened by what he'd done and the certain consequences, the doctor didn't seek aid during the hour it took for Dawson to bleed to death. He could have walked out into the street or asked someone to summon a police officer or another doctor. He could have explained when the officer knocked at his door, asking if all was well.

Instead, after the curious officer left, McDow knew he couldn't stand around fretting. His next actions weren't those of an educated professional man but, rather, of a man with a lot to lose and no good idea how to save himself.

He threw Dawson's cane and hat into the privy in the back garden. He pried up the wooden floorboards under the exterior stairs that led to the second-floor living quarters. The space under the stairs was confined and squat, but he dug as best he could into the sand to make a hole before he dragged the unwieldy body outside from his office. He hadn't dug deep enough, and the body wouldn't fit in the small hole. So he dragged it back to his examining room and tried to brush the gray, clinging sand from Captain Dawson's hair and clothes. He retrieved the cane from the privy, cleaned it and then returned his pistol to his desk drawer.

To his lover—the one who'd been upstairs visiting his wife when they heard the gunshot—he confessed what he'd done. Then he drove his buggy along the street until he saw a police officer and admitted that he'd just killed Captain Dawson.

Dr. McDow's murder trial provided the kind of distractions, puzzles and surprises that make for a headline crime, featuring the tall, distinguished longtime civic leader and war hero and the slight, quiet doctor with questionable morals.

McDow's defense attorneys knew their client didn't have the best reputation. Authors Williams and Hoffius succinctly summed up the challenges the attorneys faced in defending him:

Built on the site of the original state capital, the Charleston County Courthouse at 82–86 Broad Street is still in use. *Courtesy of Jack Boucher, Historic American Buildings Survey, Library of Congress.*

> *He had been blackballed by the local medical society, and one South Carolina newspaper reported that he was "known in almost every bawdy house in the city." There was no telling when his name might be publicly linked to the grave-robbing scandal, and one of the key witnesses to the murder, Julia Smith, was also his mistress. McDow had tried to bribe his brother to kill his wife and father-in-law, and there were police reports to prove it.*

But plenty of Charleston's poor folks stood behind McDow as a doctor willing to treat them even if they couldn't pay. The jury, as it turned out, had a strong sampling of poor, working-class citizens on it.

The witness that caused the most stir in the courtroom was Hélène Burdayron, who identified herself as Marie. Described as "the lady in black" by news reporters, she refused to directly admit that anything untoward had happened with Dr. McDow, though when confronted by reports of the surveillance on her and McDow and asked if she thought he took her to a house on Bee Street to "play croquet with him," she said, "I did not suppose so."

The trial opened in a sweltering Charleston courtroom on Monday, June 24, 1889, just over a month after Captain Dawson's death. The only question was whether McDow shot him in self-defense, as he claimed.

On Friday, after closing arguments, the jury of seven Black men and five white men retired and took a first vote. They were unanimous: Dr. McDow was not guilty. After their quick vote, they stayed behind closed doors for a couple of hours, for appearance's sake.

As Williams and Hoffius explored in their book, fortunes change quickly in the court of public opinion. Neither Dawson nor McDow were Charleston natives, but Captain Francis Dawson had worked for the betterment of Charleston, including taking some unpopular stances supporting Blacks. Dr. Thomas McDow left behind him a trail of shady dealings, but he'd been willing to treat indigent medical patients. Subtleties in their character and actions and the shifts in public sentiment marked the legacies of the key players as much as the trial did. Captain Dawson had lost some popular support because of recent political stances in his paper; he wasn't as revered as he once was, and Dr. McDow walked free—physically if not, perhaps, mentally.

Though accounts say he died in bed at the age of fifty-one, Williams and Hoffius report that Thomas McDow died by suicide in July 1904 and was buried in Magnolia Cemetery. The love triangle would have made a saucy novel, but as lived in real life, it became tawdry and tragic.

3

SERIAL AND SPREE KILLERS

The Folly Beach Killer

When does a killer become a "serial killer"? The most accepted definition of a *serial killer* requires at least two victims, with the killings separated in time or with a cooling-off period, distinguished from a *mass murderer*, who kills multiple victims in a single event, or a *spree killer*, a category harder to define but whose multiple killings are separate but with no interim "cooling off" period.

For serial killings, the oft-cited magic number of three victims originated in a federal statute setting the threshold at which the FBI can aid local law enforcement in an investigation involving multiple victims. But as the FBI stated in a 2005 symposium report from its Behavioral Analysis Unit, three victims "was not intended to be a generic definition for serial murder." Academic researchers of serial killers have set a minimum number of victims anywhere from two to ten.

Serial killers fascinate because their rapacious need to kill defies understanding. To kill in anger or when drunk or stoned, for greed or revenge, to keep someone quiet—those seem "normal" motives for murder. Those murderers tend to limit themselves to a single target. While most people can't see themselves becoming angry, fixated, greedy or frightened enough to kill, most can at least understand what drove someone to kill in such a circumstance.

But what of the killers who stalk or groom victims, first one, then another and another? Maybe they have a type of victim or a particular area where they hunt. Maybe they do it to steal or collect insurance, or maybe it's for thrills or sexual gratification. Serial killers fascinate because they are harder to understand. What makes them tick? What caused them to become so depraved? Can we root out the reason and prevent them from killing? Can we protect ourselves from becoming victims? Answers seem elusive.

On Wednesday, May 23, 1973, two young teens headed out on a walk and never returned. Nowhere could they have felt safer than Folly Beach, a quiet island scarcely six miles long and half mile wide in spots, full of vacation rentals and single-family homes. The narrow streets, the simple beach cottages, favorite breakfast spots and bars for late-night gatherings, the dunes, the beach at sunset, the slow pace of life—all attract those lucky enough to live there and those who have vacationed there for decades or for only a single, fondly remembered trip. No one could expect island residents thirteen-year-old Alexis Ann Latimer and fourteen-year-old Sherri Jan Clark to disappear from the Latimers' cottage on a hot, sunny spring afternoon.

The police just shrugged when Alexis Ann's mom called to report them missing. Kids get distracted and miss curfew or run away from home, looking

Sign welcoming visitors to Folly Beach. *Courtesy of Bre Smith via Unsplash.*

for adventure or to escape something for a while. They usually come back. Violent crime was rare on Folly Beach, and "island time" was the officers' reaction; they didn't do much to look for the girls for another two weeks. This was long before milk carton photos or on-scene advisers arriving from the National Center for Missing and Exploited Children, long before brigades of friends stapled "missing" posters to telephone poles and posted pleas for help on social media. After all, what could happen to two young teens on tranquil, funky, set-on-vacation-time Folly Beach?

As months passed, the parents stopped waiting for official help. They did what they could, handing out fliers and putting ads in the local papers. But they couldn't find their girls.

Over the next year, scattered over North Charleston, James Island and Folly Beach, different law enforcement agencies got reports of unusual assaults. A nineteen-year-old partying near the naval base brought a man home who tied her up; another teenager was gagged and tied to a tree behind a shopping center; another walking home along Folly Beach's Center Street never arrived at her house; three sixteen-year-old girls were bound and gagged and hidden in the utility room of a Folly Beach cottage. What linked such disparate cases spread over so many locations around Charleston couldn't be clear at first, especially given the limits of communications technology.

On April 12, 1974, the three girls who had been kidnapped on Folly Beach gave the police an eyewitness description of the man who took them. The three teens had played hooky from school and drove from Summerville to work on their tans at Folly Beach. The section of the beach was deserted on that spring day when a man pulled a gun on them, telling them he'd killed two policemen and they'd better do what he said or he'd kill them. He forced them to a nearby beachfront cottage and into the exterior shower room underneath the raised cottage, the kind normally used to wash the sand off after a trip to the beach. He bound them with clothesline cord, gagged them and left. Eventually, one managed to loosen her gag and started screaming. Fortunately, a police officer responding to another call on the beach heard her and discovered the captives.

The girls provided a detailed description and worked with police to create a composite drawing of a man with a mustache and beard and a distinctive birthmark on his ankle. Police widely distributed the composite, keeping quiet about the birthmark. When the case hit the newspaper, E.D. Pickerall, a beach regular, called his friend John Wilbanks, the Folly Beach city manager; in March, Pickerall had been walking the beach when his

Postcard circa 1925 of businesses at Arctic Avenue and Center Street on Folly Beach. *Courtesy of Tichnor Brothers via Boston Public Library and Wikimedia Commons.*

dog began digging in a spot full of maggots and what looked like blood. At the time, Pickerall thought someone had buried some trash or something had washed up on the beach—the kind of thing dogs find fascinating. After hearing about the three kidnapped girls, he began wondering. The house where they were found was close to that spot.

Pickerall and Wilbanks began digging in the sand and uncovered clothing. As in most small towns, they knew people who knew people. They asked another local to bring his bulldozer to push away more earth. About two feet into the sand, they found almost skeletonized remains bound with nylon clothesline rope—the same type of rope used on the girls found in the shower room and to bind the girl to a tree on James Island. The body was later identified as Mary Earline Bunch, who'd disappeared on February 20, 1974, about one week after the girl near the James Island shopping center was found alive. Sixteen-year-old Mary was last seen walking on Center Street on her two-block trip to her house. At the time, as with Alexis and Sherri, officials assumed she was a runaway and would eventually decide to come home.

As the search and excavation of the beach and dunes surrounding Mary's makeshift grave continued, neighbors stood vigil with a mix of curiosity and fear. Would they find out what happened to Alexis Ann Latimer and Sherri Jan Clark, who disappeared almost a year earlier? What had been seemingly random events spread over several small Charleston-area jurisdictions were now cause for fear. Life had changed for everyone, not just for the families and friends of the girls involved. Author Joseph C. Fisher, who lived on the island and witnessed the search of the beach, had previously lived in Michigan when a serial killer preyed on co-eds at the University of Michigan and nearby Eastern Michigan University. Those experiences prompted him to later research and write a book about how serial killings affect a community's sense of safety and trust, how preoccupation with the crimes "seemed to dominate every social interaction and to creep into and control every conversation." Residents and visitors on Folly Beach couldn't help but be preoccupied. Someone on the island was harming young girls.

After the discovery of Mary Bunch's body and the three kidnapped girls who'd survived, police canvassed the neighboring houses. They set up a roadblock and questioned drivers on the only bridge that linked Folly Beach and the mainland. Navy jets equipped with infrared sensors flew aerial sweeps over the beach, the dense vegetation and the clustered backyards. Within days of the release of the girls' description and

Folly Beach homes with tidal seagrass. *Courtesy of Doug Anderson via Flickr.*

composite drawing of their kidnapper, another witness came forward—the woman who'd been attacked after a party in North Charleston. She saw the sketch and went to notify naval officials because she believed the man worked on the base.

From the navy's personnel records, they put a name to the face: thirty-one-year-old Richard Valenti. He served as a radar operator on the crew of a rescue submarine. And he lived in the rental house across the street from where Mary Bunch's body was found.

Investigators recognized Richard Valenti as one of the neighbors who'd stood on the dunes watching the excavation and search for the body on the beach. He'd offered drinks to the searchers and encouraged his neighbors not to worry. Investigators had no doubt about the identification; officers had held back the description of a unique birthmark on the killer's ankle—a mark like one on Richard Valenti's ankle.

Ten minutes after Valenti's interrogation began at 6:40 p.m., he confessed everything, starting with the attempted sexual assault after the naval base party, followed by the kidnappings and finally describing the kidnapping and killing of Mary Bunch, Alexis Ann Latimer and Sherri Jan Clark. He'd committed his entire roster of crimes in less than a year. Two hours after his confession began, he was leading investigators to the spot where he'd buried Alexis and Sherri and the place where he'd held them: in the ground-floor shower room at a vacant rental house near where he lived. Investigators found pieces of rope still hanging from the water pipes.

At first, neighbors, colleagues and church friends were stunned to hear about the nice Bible-reading guy they thought they knew. At trial, his wife testified that she thought his violent tendencies—the result of his dysfunctional upbringing—had been tempered after they moved to Charleston and they both started attending church. But she also told of his strange bondage fetishes.

The Charleston County medical examiner reported that the two girls died from strangulation. When first interrogated by police, Valenti repeatedly attempted to distance himself from what happened. He said he'd hoped, after first seeing them on the beach, that they wouldn't still be there when he returned with his gun to kidnap them. He claimed he'd bound the two girls to overhead water pipes as they stood on a chair, but in their struggles, they'd tipped the chair over and hanged themselves. He said a part of him wanted to help them as they struggled. Instead of helping, though, he described watching them die, and medical testimony supported strangulation as the cause of death. Because of the heinousness of the acts and the aggravating circumstance of kidnapping, the prosecutor felt the crimes merited the death penalty, but at the time, the state's death penalty statute had been ruled unconstitutional.

Given the amount of news coverage that such brutal, vicious crimes against such young victims garnered, Valenti's defense fought hard—but unsuccessfully—to have the trial moved or delayed and sought to question prospective jurors closely about their prejudices and preconceived notions about his guilt. On appeal, the state's supreme court found that the judge had carefully examined the jury pool and held that "the information which the jurors had attained from the news media concerned uncontradicted facts." The only pretrial opinion piece published had extended sympathy to the families but hadn't vilified the accused. The questions for the jury to answer weren't whether the girls were dead or how they died, but whether Valenti had committed the crimes and whether he was insane, so the court appropriately kept the trial in Charleston County.

Valenti said he'd confessed to investigators because "he well remembered being promised psychiatric care if he would give a statement." The defense pushed for a change in the state's requirements for insanity pleas, but that was also denied. For years, South Carolina's legal test for insanity was the M'Naghten rule, based on an 1843 English case and adopted by the state in 1886. Under the M'Naghten rule, a defendant is insane and can't stand trial if, at the time of the act, "he has such a defect of reason, from disease of the mind" that he doesn't know that what he's doing is wrong. The M'Naghten rule is the toughest of the legal tests for establishing insanity because it requires serious cognitive impairment.

In 1982, in a tide-shifting case, John Hinckley was acquitted by reason of insanity for his attempted assassination of President Ronald Reagan and was sent to a mental hospital rather than prison. The resulting public outrage stifled attempts to move toward new, more nuanced standards for assessing criminal insanity. The debate about how to handle mentally ill criminal defendants continues, but in Valenti's case, the M'Naghten rule meant insanity wasn't a viable defense. The court found neither his sexual perversions nor his dysfunctional upbringing allowed Richard Valenti to avoid the consequences of his criminal actions.

His trial began on June 24, 1974, and lasted for four days. The solicitor closed the state's case by playing the recording of Valenti's detailed, unapologetic confession. The Charleston jury took less than an hour to convict him of murdering Alexis and Sherri. He received two life sentences.

After that verdict, he was not tried for kidnapping the three girls on Folly Beach, the girl on James Island or the woman in North Charleston, all of whom survived, or for the kidnapping and murder of Mary Bunch, age sixteen. The prosecution brought its strongest case first. Bringing no further prosecutions saved the victims and families from the ordeal of a trial.

Under state law at the time, Valenti's life sentences allowed him a parole hearing every two years after his tenth year. Each time, his parole application faced sizable opposition. Petitions were circulated, and family, friends, concerned citizens and law enforcement made the trek to Columbia to oppose his release at each of those hearings.

In December 2020, Richard Valenti died at age seventy-seven, forty-six years after his conviction. He'd been denied parole in twenty-one hearings. The prison system did not release a cause of death, stating only that it was not COVID-related.

Starting Over

What's known as South Carolina's Grand Strand or simply "the beach" covers sixty miles, from the North Carolina state line near Calabash and the mouth of the Little River south to Winyah Bay in Georgetown County. Toward the southern end of that touristy strip of vacation homes, motels, beachwear shops and pancake houses lies Murrells Inlet, a quieter, more residential area about ten miles south of Myrtle Beach proper. For anyone driving along Highway 17, Murrells Inlet would be one of the last places to expect a fledgling serial killer to operate. Even less likely would be a killer who used a branch library as his hunting ground.

In 2005, forty-three-year-old Laura Ling worked as a research librarian for the Horry County Library's Socastee Branch, about ten miles inland from Murrells Inlet. Her daughter, Christina, age fifteen, lived with her while her two sons lived with their father. Over a period of several months, Laura had gotten to know a frequent library patron named Stephen Stanko. He introduced himself as a published author who was researching and writing a new book, and she was happy to be his guide to the library's resources. He made no secret that he was an ex-con—white-collar crime, he always emphasized—now pursuing an interest in prison reform.

The two were soon dating, and within two months of meeting, Stephen asked if he could move in with Laura and her daughter. He was being evicted from his apartment and needed somewhere to land as he searched for a new place to live.

He dreamed of life as a famous writer. With two college professors, he'd co-written a book about prison life and followed that up with his autobiography and a novel or two, though those hadn't yet found publishers. For his next endeavor, perhaps he would write a comprehensive book about famous serial killers? Sitting in the library, he read and made copious notes on highly publicized murderers, but his grandiose publishing plans weren't materializing. Stephen Stanko was, at heart, a con artist. In the past, he'd proven he could persuasively spin tales and take money—typically from women. But nothing much came of the big ideas he bragged about.

While Stephen made some effort to be useful around her house, Laura soon knew he needed to leave. In April 2005, he got fired from his sales job because he wasn't closing enough deals. At the library, he set up a makeshift office and began holding himself out as a lawyer, offering advice. He had managed to insert himself into Laura Ling's home and work life and was now a liability for her on both fronts.

On April 7, her attempt to evict her freeloading boyfriend got ugly.

That day, his violent physical attack on Laura and then on her teenaged daughter, Christina, was prolonged and vicious. In the end, the six-foot, three-inch-tall Stephen put his knee in Laura's back and strangled her to death, telling Christina, "See what you did. I really loved her." Then he slit Christina's throat twice.

Stephen took his time showering, packing a bag and searching for money, credit cards, debit cards and the keys to Laura's red Mustang. Then he went to the bank and withdrew $700, his face clearly recorded on the ATM surveillance camera.

Unfortunately for Stephen, the first stage of his crime spree hadn't gone as well as he thought. Christina was still alive and soon on the phone with 911 describing him and his getaway vehicle to the dispatcher.

The next day, on April 8, Stephen Stanko paid a visit to his seventy-four-year-old friend Henry Lee Turner. The grandfather and air force veteran lived in Conway, a drive of thirty or forty minutes from Murrells Inlet, depending on the tourist traffic. Henry had taken a computer class that Laura Ling taught for library patrons and had met Stephen Stanko through the librarian. Stephen called Henry early that morning to say he was coming to visit. He lied, telling Henry that his dad had just died and he needed someone to talk to.

Henry called to break a date with his girlfriend so he'd be available for grieving Stephen, who arrived at 4:00 a.m. They chatted and ate the fast-food breakfast that Stephen picked up for the two of them. As soon as he had an opportunity, Stephen searched Henry's house for his gun. Using a pillow for a silencer, he shot Henry while he was shaving, in the back and chest, and began searching for cash or valuables that would help fund his escape. He abandoned Laura's Mustang at Henry's trailer and left in Henry's Mazda truck, headed to Columbia on Interstate 26. He spent the evening lavishly and loudly, using Laura's and Henry's money to treat patrons at the bar in the Blue Marlin Restaurant, a couple of blocks from the South Carolina State House. Then he headed west.

That weekend, the legendary Masters Golf Tournament was being played in Augusta, Georgia. In an Augusta oyster bar, businessman Stephen Christopher, in town for the tournament, caught the eye of a woman named Dana. The couple enjoyed an evening of dining, dancing and drinking together, after which she kindly offered to let him crash on her sofa. He'd partied too hard to drive safely. She made sure she locked her bedroom door, just to be cautious.

The next morning, Stephen attended church with Dana and her parents before the couple went to Sunday lunch. Stephen wowed her with a gift:

Postcard circa 1930–45 from the Augusta National Golf Club, home of the Masters Tournament. *Courtesy of Tichnor Brothers via Boston Public Library and Wikimedia Commons.*

a gold bracelet. She found herself quickly smitten. She couldn't know the charming man had stolen the bracelet from his murdered girlfriend.

Two days later, on Tuesday, April 12, Dana's mother called. A photo of the man who'd gone to church with them on Sunday was in the newspaper, on page 5B. Police were searching for him for murder and rape.

Dana Putnum immediately called the sheriff and let him know everything she could tell them about her "Stephen Christopher." A wiretap on her phone led investigators to Stephen Stanko at the food court in an Augusta shopping mall, where he was treating himself to lunch with stolen money. Henry Turner's truck was in the mall parking lot, with the .357 magnum pistol used to kill Henry inside.

Because his journey had carried him across state lines, local authorities could call in federal assistance. A team was waiting for him when he left the mall.

As distinguished from serial killers or mass murderers (who perpetrate a single event with multiple casualties), spree killers kill two or more victims within a limited time, though that period isn't defined and may last days or weeks or months. As crime sprees go, Stephen Stanko's lasted a remarkably short four days. But in those four days, the crimes he committed were calculated and cruel—and they weren't his first criminal acts.

At Goose Creek High School, north of Charleston, young Stephen Stanko had been a bright student, but after his application to the Air Force Academy was rejected, he never managed to get traction in college or in a job. In 1992, in his mid-twenties, he had his first glancing run-in with the law for falsely taking commissions from his employer.

His long-term girlfriend finally had enough of his bullying and his big talk; she called police. She knew he'd stolen checks, jewelry and paintings from her house. But she also knew to be wary. When he got angry, a switch would flip, she said. In the past, he'd put his hands on her throat and strangled her. Police arrived at her house, but Stephen talked himself out of trouble. To add another indignity, the officer told her to leave so things could calm down—even though the house where they lived belonged to her. She had another place she could go, but he said he didn't.

Stephen's history indicated an oddly mixed personality. Even his long-term girlfriend said she at first found him creepy, but she eventually let him move in with her. He moved to Atlanta, where he soon found another woman willing to take him in for a while, and then he returned to South Carolina and convinced his old girlfriend to take him back. Those who knew him found him not only glib and charming but also self-centered and grandiose, always trying to work a con. Sometimes he presented himself as a successful businessman, sometimes as an author; he was described by some as "creepy" or with "dead eyes," but he could also convince smart, self-sufficient women that they should help him out.

In February 1996, a few months after he'd convinced his old girlfriend to let him move back in with her, he attacked her. She called 911 but canceled the request and told the dispatcher he was leaving. He then tied her up and gagged her, stole her SUV and left town. He soon called her, threatening suicide. Police traced his calls to a motel off the interstate in Greenville, South Carolina. Charges for kidnapping and aggravated assault earned him a ten-year prison sentence. He served over eight years before his release.

During his time in the South Carolina prison system, he wrote and wrote, keeping notes on everything about his experience while inside and vowing to write a book. According to one of the professors who eventually coauthored *Living in Prison: A History of the Correctional System with an Insider's*

Georgetown County Courthouse, built in 1824 and designed by Robert Mills, architect of the Washington Monument and several South Carolina courthouses. *Courtesy of Upstateherd via Wikimedia Commons.*

View, the path to publication wasn't short or easy. Stephen submitted the book in 2000, and the publishing company contacted Gordon A. Crews, a college professor from South Carolina with a background in law enforcement, to provide academic support to get it ready for publication. In 2004, after some rejection and reworking, the book was published with a third coauthor, Wayne Gillespie—two months before Stephen's release from prison.

In the book, the academic coauthors gave a brief history of the U.S. penal system. In Stephen's portion, he recounted his personal experience in sometimes minute detail. He also persisted in referring to his long-term girlfriend as his wife, which he knew irritated her. On the opening page, he wrote, "Although I had been a model student and an above-average athlete during school, in the years that followed, I did not accomplish my dreams and goals. In my mind, I was a failure, and I had reduced myself to cheating my way to fortune and fame....However, I never planned to commit a crime, and I never expected that I would ever become a criminal."

Stephen's killing spree started a year after his book's publication. One of his coauthors reported getting calls from CNN, Nancy Grace, Fox News, MSNBC and *Good Morning America*, among others. As part of a 2011 academic presentation on criminology given in Kobe, Japan, the professor told the audience, "The producer from the *Today Show* called to say that if he killed again and/or was gone longer than a week, they would have me on!"

Stephen's short spree didn't provide the national media much time to follow the story. His trial—for kidnapping, the murder of Laura Ling, the sexual assault and attempted murder of Christina—began on August 7, 2006, in the Georgetown County Courthouse. His defense lawyers argued that he was insane, his brain congenitally damaged and aggravated by an old head injury that left him unable to tell right from wrong—a key element of his defense. After the weeklong trial, the jury deliberated only two hours before convicting him on all charges and recommended the death penalty.

His second trial, for the murder of his friend Henry Lee Turner, started in Horry County on November 13, 2009. Even though Stanko had formally complained that his attorney was ineffective in his first trial, he unequivocally insisted that the same lawyer continue to represent him.

Henry's girlfriend testified that Stephen was at Henry's house the day of the murder—she'd talked to Henry while Stephen was visiting. After a six-day trial, the jury found him guilty, and in the penalty phase, he again received a death sentence which was upheld on appeal.

Stephen Stanko's 2024 mug shot. *Courtesy of the South Carolina Department of Corrections website.*

In the ensuing fifteen years, Stephen Stanko has spent a lot of time filing motions and appeals. In February 2022, a federal magistrate ordered that the Department of Corrections deliver him to MUSC in Charleston for brain scans. As recently as March 2024, his appellate lawyer—Joseph Perkovich, a death penalty defense lawyer in New York—argued that the insanity defense presented by Stephen's trial lawyer was ineffective and damaged his chances for a fair trial with the jury. Perkovich also argued that, even though Stephen said he wanted William Diggs to continue as his attorney in the Henry Turner trial, he had filed a motion claiming Diggs was ineffective in his first trial. Perkovich argued Diggs therefore should not have represented him in the second trial. According to Courthouse News reporter Steve Garrison, Diggs called Stephen Stanko a psychopath in front of the jury, which "didn't help explain his actions, but instead turned him into a monster." Perkovich argued that, as a result, Stephen deserved a new trial.

In July 2024, the federal Fourth Circuit Court of Appeals, in a detailed opinion, denied his new attorney's petition challenging his conviction and sentence.

At age fifty-six, Stephen Stanko remains incarcerated on South Carolina's death row unit at the Broad River Correctional Institution in Columbia, where he has been held since his initial conviction in 2006. No date has been set for his execution.

4
GIRLS JUST WANT TO HAVE FUN

RENEE POOLE

In June 1998, Brent and Renee Poole drove almost four hours from their home outside Winston-Salem, North Carolina, for a romantic three-day getaway in Myrtle Beach. The young couple were celebrating their third wedding anniversary. For many, a drive to the beach heralds a time-honored transition from home to enjoying sun, sand, seafood and quiet, lazy time with each other.

The Pooles chose an oceanfront hotel on the north end of Myrtle Beach, a quieter area away from most of the parties and crowds. About two o'clock in the morning of June 9, Renee convinced Brent to take a stroll on the beach for a romantic interlude. They walked over the dunes to the stretch of beach between Eightieth and Eighty-Second Avenues and, in a secluded spot, made love to the sound of the surf. After the thrill of avoiding detection by other late-night beachgoers, they gathered up their towel and walked along the sand back toward their hotel.

A man appeared out of the darkness. In black pants, hooded sweatshirt and gloves, he wasn't dressed for the beach on a warm June night.

He brandished a handgun, tackled Brent and forced him to the ground, straddling him to subdue him. Waving his 9mm pistol, he ordered Renee to lay down in the sand with the soles of her feet in contact with her husband's feet. Brent asked the man not to kill him, saying that he had a two-year-old daughter. The man shot Brent once in the head. The gun jammed, but on the third attempt, he shot Brent a second time, stole his watch and wallet, took Renee's engagement ring from her finger and ran toward the dune access and the road.

In shock, Renee looked for one of the beach patrol vehicles they'd seen earlier that night. She approached an officer in his truck and reported that someone had shot her husband.

Shootings in Myrtle Beach weren't unheard of; they just didn't happen this far from the clubs and night spots. Was the man still lurking nearby? Later, investigators would question her demeanor and her actions, given that she'd just witnessed her husband being shot to death.

Investigators naturally focused on her as the prime witness. They had trouble making sense of the attack, especially when, weeks later, Brent's wallet was found in a residential yard, blocks from the murder scene. The wallet was soaking wet as if it had been outside in the elements, and it still contained Brent's driver's license, debit card and a few dollars. Robbery apparently wasn't the motive.

Two witnesses later came forward, reporting they had seen a man acting suspiciously near their beachfront hotel that night. The man saw them

View from Bird Island looking across the inlet toward North Myrtle Beach. *Courtesy of Stuart Borrett via Flickr.*

watching him and walked quickly away toward the beach. Something about him lurking and trying to avoid contact spooked the wife, but the couple decided to continue their planned beach walk. When they returned, they again saw the man trying to crouch out of sight behind the hotel. When he saw them watching him, he turned away, walking parallel to but not on the beach. The couple later learned that Brent and Renee Poole had been attacked near that location. They came forward and were able to identify the man in a photo lineup—a man named John Frazier.

In the news coverage of the case, Renee Poole was always identified as an exotic dancer. She worked at the Silver Fox in Winston-Salem because she made good money. For some, though, her job raised questions about her character. Then later evidence revealed she was having an affair while her husband worked out of town as a mechanic at Mack Truck in Charlotte.

Over time, Renee had started confiding in John Frazier, a regular Silver Fox customer, about her frustrations with her husband and her marriage. She wanted out, but she didn't want to share custody of their daughter—and she didn't want to lose out on his company pension plan or his $100,000 life insurance policy. Renee loved nice things, which was why she insisted on dancing at the club. She also found she liked John Frazier's attentiveness, how he lit her cigarettes and opened car doors for her. He listened while she complained about Brent's carelessness with money, his debt and his reliance on his mother.

Renee and John Frazier became lovers. And she began imagining the possibility of a better life for herself and her daughter.

During Renee's initial interview with police on June 12, her lawyer was present. But the following day, she gave a second lengthy interview without her counsel. In that statement, she admitted that she and John Frazier had planned her husband's murder. Only later would questions arise about the reliability of that confession.

Both Renee and John were extradited from North Carolina for separate trials in Horry County. Court TV would record the proceedings.

The prosecution, led by solicitor (and later state senator) Greg Hembree and assistant solicitor Fran Humphries, contended that Renee was the criminal mastermind driving the plot. Without her instigation and cooperation, John Frazier wouldn't have killed Brent Poole. At trial, a neighbor testified that he saw John Frazier's black Chevrolet Blazer parked at the Pooles' house every day while Brent was at work in Charlotte over a three-month period. Their affair—and probably their planning—had continued for a few months.

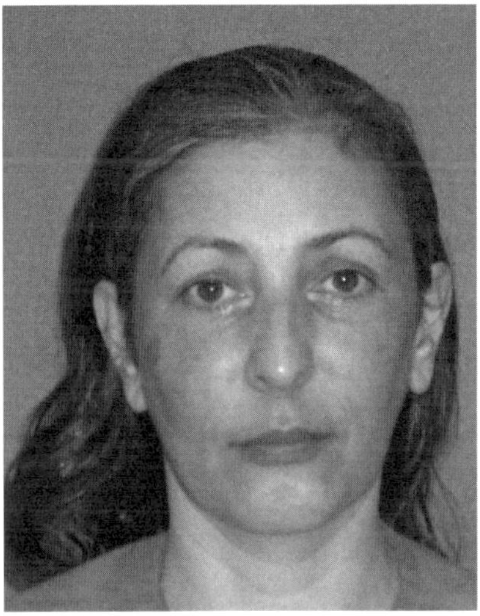

Mug shots of Renee Poole and John Boyd Frazier, 2024. *Courtesy of the South Carolina Department of Corrections website.*

Renee's statements, contradictions and admissions to police would be the heart of the case against her—and the source of continuing questions about the fairness of the verdict.

For the defense, Dr. Tony Albiniak, a psychology professor at nearby Coastal Carolina University, testified about why innocent people make false confessions during police interrogation. Under ordinary circumstances, the notion of confessing guilt when you'd done nothing wrong seems ludicrous. However, a lengthy interrogation, physical and mental stress, threats if they don't confess, promises if they do—all increase the odds of eliciting a confession to something that didn't happen. Dr. Albiniak had studied the research, taught classes and written papers on false confessions for over a decade. In reviewing the hours of Renee's interrogation, he identified fifteen different points where police used the kinds of tactics or questions that researchers say most often elicit false confessions.

Dr. Albiniak wasn't able to make a complete assessment because Renee's lawyers wouldn't let him interview her; he relied only on the police interviews. On cross-examination, the prosecution got Dr. Albiniak to admit that he'd never even met Renee or examined her. They argued that, as a result, he shouldn't be allowed to testify about the validity of her confession. The judge disagreed and allowed the testimony.

The questions raised about false confessions apparently didn't sway the jurors. She was convicted of murder and criminal conspiracy by a Horry County jury on November 13, 1999.

On February 14, 2000, John Frazier stood trial, with a defense team that had cost his mother almost half a million dollars up to that point. His defense brought to court a recorded deposition by renowned psychologist Dr. Elizabeth Loftus from Seattle, an expert in faulty eyewitness accounts. She would have called into question the reliability of the testimony from the couple who put John at the scene of the murder, but the judge refused to allow the jury to hear that evidence. On appeal, Frazier won a new trial based on the judge blocking parts of Dr. Loftus's testimony and other evidence questioning the eyewitness testimony.

Ultimately, though, John Frazier was convicted and sentenced to thirty years for armed robbery, criminal conspiracy and murder. His projected release date is November 19, 2029.

Neither Renee nor John testified against the other.

In 2018, eighteen years after Renee was sent to prison without the possibility of parole, a new lawyer found enough questions about Renee's confession to police and about her initial trial to appeal her conviction. Charles Grose, an experienced defense lawyer from Greenwood, agreed to represent her in an appeal without compensation because he saw "interesting things about her case that needed to be addressed," according to an interview with journalist Kathy Ropp. Grose contended that Renee's confession was not voluntary because police pressured her during her interviews by lying to her, threatening to take her daughter and violating her constitutional right to remain silent. During her jury's deliberations, one juror had been uncertain about whether they had to accept her confession just because the judge had allowed it into evidence if they believed it was illegally obtained. The note from the juror asking that question was never given to the judge; however, the court of appeals held that failure to have the judge explain how they should treat their doubts about the questioned police tactics was not a prejudicial error.

In 2001, J.L. Hardee, the juror who had doubts during Renee's trial, published a book about his experience serving on the jury. In particular, he was concerned that the detectives who questioned her testified that they didn't suspect her until *after* she confessed. They said that was why they hadn't given her a Miranda warning before they questioned her. They didn't remind her, before they questioned her for hours, that she could stay silent and had a right to counsel. Juror Hardee didn't find it believable that she wasn't a suspect and felt she should have been given the constitutionally required warning. He also said the lack of direct evidence against her concerned him and other jurors—they remained split six to six during several hours of deliberation and, at the end, felt forced to arrive at a verdict, no matter what.

Hardee regretted voting for conviction. In his opinion, Renee "wasn't found guilty because the jury thought she committed this crime. She was found guilty because she was a stripper, she cheated on her husband, and we were ready to go home." He wrote that if he'd had to endure the hours of questioning that Renee did, he probably would have told them anything they wanted to hear.

Despite efforts of those who continue to raise questions about how her confession was obtained and the fairness of her prosecution, Renee continues to serve her life sentence without the possibility of parole.

5
CRIME FIRSTS

The First DNA Case

A small town where families have lived for generations, where kids visit swimming holes or backyard pools, have summer barbeques or fish fries, water ski or fish or hunt together and gather for Friday night high school football or to celebrate graduations—Conway was that kind of town.

As with the other coastal counties in South Carolina, Horry County remained isolated and self-contained until roads and bridges improved transportation over the wetlands and rivers that cut through the area. Now, nineteen million beachgoers pass through Conway every year on the way to their beach week or weekend getaway.

Bonnie Faye Todd grew up in Horry County, watching its changes and growing pains. Crystal Faye Todd was her only daughter, and Bonnie Faye had mostly raised her alone. Her husband had died while Crystal was young. The two were friends as well as mother and daughter, and seventeen-year-old Crystal appreciated how hard her mother worked to provide for her and raise her.

At 3:30 a.m. on Sunday morning, November 17, 1991, Bonnie Faye called Horry County's 911 dispatcher. Crystal had gone to a party that evening and still wasn't home, though her mother expected her home no later than 12:30 a.m. Crystal was outgoing, loved parties and visiting with her friends on the phone and in person. But staying out so late and worrying her mother wasn't something Crystal would do. Bonnie Faye described for the dispatcher the new blue Toyota Celica that Crystal was driving, a high school graduation present she had given her daughter.

As the early morning hours passed, Bonnie Faye called around to Crystal's friends, trying to find her or anyone who might know where she was. She was frantic. She called 911 again at 8:00 a.m. and told them she was certain her daughter was dead, that they needed to do something. Before 9:00 a.m., a county police officer went to the Todds' home and took a formal missing person's report. Even though the distraught mother knew this was more than a daughter who'd lost track of time or fallen asleep on a friend's couch, police took a more dispassionate view. They'd seen teenagers return home the next morning with a lot of explaining to do but safe and unharmed.

At 9:10 a.m. that Sunday morning, less than half an hour after the officer took Bonnie Faye's missing person report, 911 dispatch received another call. Two men headed out deer hunting were driving down a dirt road in rural Horry County when one spotted blood on the road. Thinking someone had killed a deer, he got out to examine the spot. Seemed a lot of blood for a deer kill. They followed drag marks to a ditch with a five-foot-high bank and found the bruised and bloody body of a young woman. Even when an EMT arrived who knew the missing Crystal Todd, he couldn't conclusively identify her. The brutal attack left her with bruises, abrasions, more than thirty stab wounds and her throat cut deeply; she'd been sexually assaulted and disemboweled. Whoever viciously attacked Crystal didn't intend for her survive.

As word spread among family, church members and friends of Crystal's, they started arriving at Bonnie Faye's house outside Conway. Everyone knew losing Crystal would devastate her. Losing her to some unnamed monster only compounded the mother's loss and grief. One of the earliest visitors was stocky, athletic Ken Register. He lived close by, and he and Crystal had grown up together. They'd dated for a short while but remained good friends. Eighteen-year-old Ken, who had graduated from Conway High School the year before Crystal, became one of Bonnie Faye's stalwarts. He served as one of Crystal's pallbearers at her funeral, and he visited Bonnie and commiserated with her over the months as investigators tried to find out who could have killed her daughter.

Investigators learned that around 11:00 p.m. on Saturday, November 16, Crystal was in the parking lot of Coastal Mall talking with one of her girlfriends. Later, Crystal's car was found parked at Conway Middle

School. No one reported seeing her getting into someone else's car or any sighting of her since shortly after eleven o'clock. She'd just disappeared.

Local officers requested assistance from the State Law Enforcement Division (SLED), which can provide investigative expertise, staffing and resources that smaller jurisdictions lack. The forensics lab at SLED in Columbia would analyze evidence taken from the scene and from the autopsy conducted at the Medical University of South Carolina in Charleston.

Meanwhile, slowly and methodically, Horry County investigators interviewed the list of those who knew Crystal, who went to school with or worked with her, anyone who'd been in her circle. On January 13, 1992, two months into the investigation, SLED agents took a statement from her childhood friend Ken Register. They wanted to know what he could tell them about her habits, her boyfriends, anything that might give them a lead. When they asked where he'd been the night Crystal disappeared and died, Ken had an alibi with plenty of witnesses: he was with his girlfriend at the Dodge City Park Raceway, a go-kart track in Aynor, a small town about fifteen miles from Conway. Ken also agreed to provide biologic samples: blood, saliva, hairs, finger and palm prints—whatever he could do to help. He was sample number fifty-two, the last one on their list of Crystal's close associates they had to check.

In 1992, Ken Register was likely one of millions of people unfamiliar with DNA—and unfamiliar with what DNA could reveal. The field of forensic DNA was still very new. Even when a lab fast-tracked a sample, test results could take weeks or months to analyze. The television program *CSI* wouldn't debut until more than eight years later, in October 2000. Few people knew what the initials DNA stood for, and few people expected microscopic evidence commonly known only by its initials to be able to seal a killer's fate. But the lab identified nine bands that matched Ken's DNA with the semen left on Crystal's body. At trial, an expert testified "that previously the most bands observed to match between two individuals had been three out of nine and, therefore, it was extraordinary to observe a nine-band match of five separate pieces of DNA."

The likelihood that this same pattern would occur in the general population was 1 in 250 million. As the science of DNA analysis progressed, technology could more accurately separate mixtures of DNA and identify the separate contributors to a sample, and "matches" in the millions and trillions became commonplace. But the numbers they found in the samples on Crystal's body were more than enough. On January 18, 1992, five days after his initial meeting with law enforcement, officers met Ken Register arrived at his workplace. They asked him to read and acknowledge his Miranda rights. Ken asked twice, while he was being taken to the police station, if he could see his mother.

For about three hours, investigators questioned Ken at the station. As they were permitted by law to do, they lied about the evidence they'd collected against him over the two months since Crystal's death. Investigators are allowed to tell a suspect they've found things they haven't found. In truth, the scene along the dirt farm road hadn't yielded tire or shoe tracks. They had, however, found one irrefutable, incontrovertible piece of evidence: they had his DNA from semen on Crystal's body.

According to court records, Ken refused to say anything "about it" and insisted he had to talk to his mother first. The investigators ended their session with Ken and took an hour's break to visit his mother's house. She didn't return to the station with them but wrote a note for them to take back to her son: "Ken, I love you. I know where you were at. We know when you left the race track and I know when you got home. I'll stand by you. I love you! Mama."

Those questioning Ken didn't want to hand him a note in which his mother reminded him she could give him an alibi. Instead, when they rejoined Ken in the interview room, they told him his mama was upset, she loved him and "she wanted him to tell them 'what happened that night.'" They continued talking to him about his family and his girlfriend. Half an hour later, at about 3:00 p.m., he confessed to killing Crystal.

Ken hadn't agreed to a tape recording of their session or of his confession, so they gave him a written statement to sign. On more than one occasion, he was read or asked to read and acknowledge that he understood his Miranda rights, that he didn't have to talk to them and that he could have a lawyer.

Ken Register's case appeared before the state's supreme court even before it could go to trial. On July 6, 1992, the appellate court heard arguments about whether Ken's current fifteen-year-old girlfriend, who was called Jane Doe in the documents to keep her identity private, could be required to provide samples of her hair, blood and saliva for DNA testing. The prosecution had requested the testing because Ken claimed that hair and fluids found in his car were the result of having sex with his girlfriend; the prosecution wanted to be able to rebut that claim at trial. DNA testing was relatively new and untried in South Carolina courts, and the state supreme court's detailed opinion demonstrated an understanding that what this new technology would bring in the future could not be forecast: "It is impossible to set forth a rigid test to be applied in all circumstances," the opinion read. The factors must "remain flexible." The court order denied the prosecution's request for biologic evidence from the girlfriend without a clearer showing of probable cause or relationship to the defendant's guilt.

At the 1992 trial, Solicitor Ralph Wilson prosecuted the case. He'd begun his courtroom training as a public defender before joining the solicitor's office. His candidacy had been endorsed by his former boss, legendary Horry County solicitor Jim Dunn, and in 1990, he was elected the first African American solicitor in the state.

Tensions were high in the courtroom as families who'd been longtime friends faced each other and fought for their children. But interest in the case wasn't limited to Horry County. DNA didn't become a household word until the O.J. Simpson trial opened in 1994. This was DNA's first test in a South Carolina court, though this was far from the first case where DNA linked a defendant to a murder. The first conviction was in England in 1986; in that case, DNA freed the initial suspect in the murders of two children before it helped convict the real killer, Colin Pitchfork. In the

Horry County Courthouse, built in 1908. *Courtesy of TheDigitel via Flickr.*

United States, the 1987 Southside Strangler case in Virginia was the first capital murder conviction using DNA; it inspired Patricia Cornwell's novel *Postmortem*, published in 1990.

News outlets knew this case would attract viewers—and contrarian attacks can boost viewership even more. On January 14, 1993, CBS's *Street Stories*, with Deborah Norville, Dan Rather and Ed Bradley, asked "Did science make a mistake?" As detailed by Dale Hudson and Billy Hills in their book about the case, *An Hour to Kill*, the television program raised the specter of poor crime scene processing and shoddy science and played up the small-town nature of Conway. Norville interviewed Barry Scheck and Peter Neufeld, the DNA experts on O.J.'s defense team. They pointed out that the statistical probabilities used in DNA testing can be "misleading and misinterpreted." They also questioned the lack of national standards for testing and whether a state lab was as reliable as a private lab with more forensic DNA experience. The statement that raised hackles around Conway, though, was recounted by Hudson and Mills: "Scheck and Neufeld defined the circumstances. In a small town, where everyone is married to their cousins, it would be possible for two people to have the same DNA profile, based on shared genes. In fact, Scheck said, it was probable, in a 'small inbred town like Conway.'" Townspeople were insulted, but they were also wondering what other evidence the prosecution had against Ken Register.

Some of their questions were answered on the first day of trial. The initial witnesses described the discovery of Crystal's body in the ditch and her horrifying injuries. That afternoon, two detectives testified about Ken's arrest and his confession. On cross-examination, Ken's attorney Morgan Martin tore into the detectives about their tactics, challenging that they "got him isolated, you got him scared."

"I didn't get him into anything," Detective Bill Knowles countered. "What he got, he got himself into."

In defending Ken, his attorneys called several witnesses that placed him at the go-kart track at the time Crystal disappeared. They attacked the DNA evidence in pretrial hearings and in cross-examining the state's witnesses. But their principal point of attack was the validity of his confession. They called Dr. Richard Ofshe, a sociology professor at the University of California at Berkeley. The expert worked through the common elements of a false confession for the jury. In particular, the detective who questioned Ken tried and failed to get Ken to corroborate key parts of his confession, even though, Dr. Ofshe said, the detective "did a professional job in attempting to elicit it." In Dr. Ofshe's opinion, Ken Register's confession was a "coerced compliant confession."

After the defense rests its case, the state can call rebuttal witnesses to address issues presented by defense witnesses. In rebuttal, the prosecution called Dr. Park Dietz, a forensic psychiatrist who had testified in the celebrity trials of President Reagan's shooter, John Hinckley Jr., and Jeffrey Dahmer, as well as other serial killers and mass murderers. In many of his courtroom appearances, Dietz testified for the prosecution, and his practiced, knowledgeable teaching style was usually persuasive.

According to Dr. Dietz, "An unreliable confession is one that's contradicted by other facts or where a defendant contradicts himself by telling different stories at different times." In this case, Dietz pointed out where the evidence and the confession agreed, without contradiction. Solicitor Wilson asked why someone would admit to murder but refuse to admit to other things related to the crime. In this case, the detective questioning Ken had asked what happened to the knife, Crystal's car keys, the buttons from her shirt, his bloody clothes and other elements.

Dietz responded that some details "would, of course, make a murderer sound more extreme, would make a killer sound more evil and would reveal perversions that a guilty party would be ashamed to admit." Especially in cases of sexual assault, revealing details "would make them less of a man in the eyes of those they're talking to, and they don't want to admit that. They're ashamed of it."

After deliberating less than five hours, the jury found Ken Register guilty of murder, first-degree criminal sexual conduct and kidnapping. In South Carolina, a first-degree murder conviction with an aggravating circumstance—which includes kidnapping or sexual assault—makes the defendant eligible for the death penalty. After a conviction, the jury would then hear additional evidence and decide a suitable punishment. In the penalty phase of the trial, the solicitor was allowed to introduce evidence that Ken exposed himself to two college students two months before the murder and that Ken terrorized a young woman in dozens of anonymous phone calls with references to sexual assault, mutilation and murder—the very indignities, argued the solicitor, that Crystal suffered. The furious young woman had notified the police, who tried to trace the calls. Eventually, through her own detective work, she tracked the calls back to a fifteen-year-old Ken Register, whom she'd met when she visited his uncle's car repair shop.

The prosecution also called Dr. Robert Hazelwood, one of the founders of the FBI's behavioral profiling program and an expert in sexually violent crimes. The defense successfully objected to any testimony about profiling because many innocent people may have characteristics found in a profile; matching those characteristics doesn't make a person guilty. But the judge allowed Dr. Hazelwood to testify in his area of expertise: sexual sadism and sexual homicide.

In the penalty phase, the jury deliberated for an hour and fifteen minutes. They found Ken Register guilty with aggravating circumstances but recommended life in prison rather than the death penalty. He received a life sentence for murder and the associated kidnapping, plus thirty years for first-degree criminal sexual conduct and five years for other charges.

Ken and his family had numerous supporters, including Mickey Spillane—a longtime beach resident famous for his hardboiled detective novels—and his wife, Jane. Contradictory testimony and new science didn't convince everyone.

As recently as February 2024, thirty years after his conviction, Ken Register petitioned for a parole hearing and was denied. Crystal's family had fought to keep him in prison at past hearings, and as they'd pledged to Bonnie Faye before her death, they continued, gathering signatures on an online petition. Under South Carolina law at the time of his sentencing, Ken is eligible for a parole hearing every two years. Crystal's cousin told Ashley Listrom, a WMBF news reporter, "It's just hard because you suppress the emotions, but when that parole hearing comes up, you have to relive those feelings again."

The First Female Serial Killer?

The legends that grow up around centuries-old crime cases seldom have more than a kernel of truth in them. The dearth of confirmable facts and the overlay of modern perception on a distant pass embellish stories sometimes beyond recognition. Still, something about the tale invariably has kept it alive and in the imaginations of listeners far removed from the time and place of its origin. And usually, the best tales carry a moral among the dusty fragments of what really happened.

An engraving of Charleston in 1850. *Courtesy of artist John W. Hill and the New York Public Library Digital Collection.*

Such is the story of Lavinia Fisher, credited with being the first female serial killer in the United States and the first woman hanged in South Carolina—neither infamy definitively true.

To set the stage, for most who lived in Charleston in the early 1800s, the beautiful mansions lining the Battery and Meeting Street had nothing to do with their lives. Charleston was a fishing and trading town with a thriving port and busy roads used by coastal plantation owners, inland farmers and upstate trappers to bring indigo, cotton, foodstuffs, pelts and other goods to market. The outskirts of Charleston were filled with pens for wagon horses and livestock brought for sale as well as public houses where travelers could get a meal and something strong to drink, maybe a bed and a place to clean up before their trek home. The people who worked with their hands and kept the state's economy moving weren't those invited to dine in the big houses. The workers supped and slept in rough taverns like Six Mile House, located near where today's Dorchester Road and Rivers Avenue meet, six miles north from Charleston on Meeting Street.

Roads where money and goods are transported have always attracted those who'd rather steal than work. "Highway robbery"—and even murder—were a real threat on lonely stretches of dirt tracks leading to and from the backcountry. Most travelers probably thought they were safe when they reached the outskirts of Charleston and its welcoming wayside taverns, but not always. Even highwaymen needed a place to feed and water their horses and to eat and rest.

The Fisher gang operated out of Six Mile House. At least two men had recently been attacked by the gang and said a woman was involved in the foray. She'd memorably put one man's head through a windowpane. The gang's crimes—or rumors of what they'd done—became so notorious that on February 18, 1819, a posse of vigilantes rode out from Charleston to capture them. In their fervor, the posse mistakenly burned Five Mile House, a tavern closer to Charleston, before they proceeded on to Six Mile House. They captured Lavinia Fisher; her husband, John; two other men; and a woman and hauled them off to the Charleston Jail on Magazine Street.

The jail was constructed in 1802 and continued operating until 1939. No running water, no heat, almost no ventilation in the baking heat and humidity, no waste removal system other than an occasional mucking out of the filth-laden straw strewn on the floor—most kept their animals in better conditions than Charleston criminals endured. Even though South Carolina led the Southern states in the number of offenses eligible for hanging (165

The Old Charleston Jail at 21 Magazine Street operated from 1802 until 1939. *Courtesy of Michael Rivera via Wikimedia Commons.*

crimes), the jail conditions were so bad that inmates were more likely to die of disease than at the end of a rope.

Measuring conditions in the old jail against modern standards isn't a fair comparison, though even the city's poorest houses had privies out back and water from a pump in the yard or down the street. As a courtesy, Lavinia and John were given a small cell together, though it was far from comfortable. The rumors at the time—and as later embellished—credited them with untold numbers of dastardly murders. Ruthless Lavinia allegedly poisoned guests at the inn. Some reported a bed that tilted and dumped hapless victims into the basement, where they were either dispatched or buried if the alleged poison had done its work. The couple was charged with assault, intent to murder and highway robbery.

Local records show that two bodies were found in the woods near Six Mile House, but they weren't linked to the Fishers or the inn. None of the peacekeepers on the raid found any sign of a deadly bed or a basement full of bones or evidence of poison. Bruce Orr, a Lowcountry native, former police detective and dogged pursuer of the facts, published *Six Miles to Charleston* in 2010, debunking many of the myths about Lavinia. She was certainly a participating member of the gang, but a serial killer? No bodies were found to prove multiple murders, even when the area was dug up decades later to build the hospital at the naval base. And she was not the first woman hanged in the United States—though sending a female to the gallows was a rarity. She was, however, uncommonly good at attracting attention.

From the first, Lavinia captivated Charleston. She and her husband were tall and handsome. However, Lavinia did not handle her incarceration with grace or bravery, and she fiercely fought to save her life. Unlike stories that hyped their criminal exploits, stories told about the time the Fishers' spent in the Charleston Jail have typically stuck with the facts, including a failed escape attempt when John got out the window and to the ground but wouldn't leave Lavinia after their blanket rope broke.

Judge Elihu Bay presided over a hearing soon after their arrest. Elderly, deaf, beset by a painful stutter, he lived in the house next to St. Michael's Churchyard that later served as the rectory, just steps from the courthouse. Even though Judge Bay tended to be sympathetic to women prisoners, that didn't help Lavinia, and the outcome of the trial was inevitable. They were found guilty of highway robbery—not murder, but still a capital crime.

As often happens in high-profile cases when the rare woman stood as defendant, the ladies of the town—those who would never have gone

Judge Elihu Bay lived at 76 Meeting Street, built in 1785; starting in 1942, it served as the rectory for St. Michael's Church. *Courtesy of Spencer Means via Flickr.*

near Six Mile House—fought to save her but failed to halt the wheels of justice.

Ministers at the time took it as their mission to convert those facing death on the gallows. Perhaps in saving that soul, they could turn others from a life doomed to destruction by eliciting what were known as gallows confessions. In the United States and in England, publishers rushed broadsides into the hands of readers who wanted lurid details of the crimes and their confessions.

Dr. Richard Furman attended the Fishers in the jail, praying with them daily and even walking with them to the gallows erected on Meeting Street at the edge of the city when the trip could be delayed no longer.

On February 18, 1820, Lavinia and John stood together, their wrists bound. For the solemn occasion, John wrote a gallows statement asserting his conversion and claiming his innocence. Lavinia didn't want to die and had to be helped up the steps. She shrieked, begged and cursed before they placed the noose over her head. Her fiery speech to those gathered was memorable and oft recounted: "Cease! I will have none of it. Save your words for others that want them. But if you have a message you want to send to hell, give it to me—I'll carry it!" Pastor Furman—for whom Furman University is named—had to feel disappointed that he'd lost one.

The Old Jail still stands, a shocking and sobering sight as it looms into view on Magazine Street, three blocks west from the King Street shopping district and a block south of the College of Charleston campus. Lavinia could technically be termed a serial killer only if she could be connected with the two bodies in the woods—but she wasn't. Stories persist that Lavinia was hanged in her wedding gown, but as author Bruce Orr pointed out, all defendants wore white shifts over their clothes.

She also wasn't the first woman hanged in the United States. Early records on judicial hangings are incomplete and were kept by local jurisdictions, not by the state. But she could well be the first woman executed in South Carolina. Not until 1943, when Sue Logue was sent to the electric chair, did the state (rather than a local government) execute a woman in South Carolina. (See *True Crime Stories of Upstate South Carolina* for Logue's story.) Even without first-place status or other embellishment, Lavinia's fiery, unwavering defiance makes her a most colorful female criminal.

6
THE UNKNOWN

Missing and Not Found

Seventy-two-year-old Ernest Vereen was a man who attracted notice. At six feet, three inches tall, with a head of thick white hair and dark-rimmed owlish glasses, he was well-known in the beach community of Garden City, just north of Murrells Inlet. Ernest's family first settled in the coastal area in the late 1800s. According to *The State* reporter John Norton, the family once "held title to the entire beachfront between Murrell's Inlet and what is now Surfside Beach." His grandfather was one of the first to build a house on the beach—not a popular choice at the time because of the risk of storm damage and the difficulty of traveling across the marshland and tidal creeks to reach the beach. Ernie, as he was known, was credited by his family with naming the Vereens' holdings "Garden City."

Over the years, the grandfather's property was divided into smaller plots inherited by the offspring. On his sixty acres, Ernie built the Garden City Mobile Home Park, a tree-shaded and spacious development where vacationers, mostly from Columbia, kept their beach homes for weekend and summer visits and where retirees settled permanently.

Ernie and his son Alan owned and operated the park, and Ernie lived in one of the mobile homes. As property values climbed, Ernie's holdings appreciated, but he remained "land poor," reinvesting earnings to maintain the park. His son Alan told reporter John Norton that Ernie remained a

An inlet surrounded by seagrass marsh at Murrell's Inlet in Georgetown County, on the southern end of the coast's Grand Strand. *Courtesy of Liz Mitchell via Flickr.*

cautious businessman, holding onto his land rather than speculating. Even though his father had a heart condition, he stayed active and involved in the business, and the park had just reached the point where it could generate enough income to live on.

About lunchtime on October 11, 1984, Alan ran into Ernie's neighbor, retired police officer Homer Furr. Homer was concerned that Ernie's car hadn't moved that day from the carport next to his house. Alan went to check and found the blinds drawn. Inside, all was quiet, except for a few things out of place in the kitchen and a glass of orange juice on the table. Those small things troubled Alan. His dad was always tidy and wouldn't have walked out leaving things out of order and his eyeglasses on the dresser. Alan couldn't find anyone who'd seen his dad since the evening before, on October 10, when he'd gotten a call that a fire had broken out in a restaurant on his property. The call proved to be bogus. Alan figured his dad just took off that morning to ride somewhere with friends and thought no more about it.

At nine o'clock that evening, Alan's phone rang. A voice claimed that Ernie had been kidnapped and told Alan to look in his mailbox for a note with instructions. Alan called the police immediately, without opening the mailbox.

The responding officer found Ernie's driver's license and a typed note demanding delivery of $250,000 in forty-eight hours.

"Your father, as you may have already guessed, is in our custody. We will know if you go to the police. It really doesn't make any difference to us if you don't corporate [*sic*]. By using you and your father as examples of what happens by not doing what we say, the next mark will be more than glad to corporate....If you want to see your father alive again and your family stay alive, just do as we say." The note's typed signature was WUO.

Alan managed to gather $75,000. Police marked the bills and photocopied them to document the serial numbers.

When the kidnapper called two days later, Alan answered the phone. In just the way a kidnapping plays out in a television drama, he was instructed to drive to a string of phone booths between Myrtle Beach and Conway, including an A&P grocery store and Conway Hospital. He wore a hidden recording device while police discreetly followed him. The instruction in the final phone call was to deposit the money in a black garbage bag behind a concrete piling on the U.S. 501 bridge over the Intracoastal Waterway.

Alan Vereen and the kidnapper weren't the only visitors to the Intracoastal Waterway bridge that night. Nineteen FBI agents were staked out near the bridge with seven additional agents in two surveillance aircraft filming the ransom pickup. At trial, jurors would watch a thirty-minute videotape of the operation. The agents observed a five-foot, seven-inch-tall man pick up the bag. Alan recognized him from their description: Alvin Owens, a fifty-two-year-old man who worked as a handyman and hooked up new mobile homes when they were delivered to the park.

For several hours, agents followed Alvin from the bridge as he stopped by different businesses in Myrtle Beach; reports said he paid off some personal debts during those stops, but published accounts differ. A later appellate court opinion said Alvin spent only $18 of the ransomed funds. Another account said Alvin spent one of the $100 bills to settle a bar tab at a local tavern. Agents followed him to his apartment and arrested him later that day.

On October 14, police executed a search warrant for Alvin's Myrtle Beach apartment and his car, where they found bills with numbers included in the ransom payment. They recovered a second cache of marked bills when Alvin's children found it underneath his nightstand. Alvin's defense lawyer would later claim that the kind of sloppy police work that missed the bills on the first search had compromised the entire investigation.

As officers gathered evidence, teams of state, local and federal law enforcement agents, along with volunteers from the military base and the community, searched for Ernie Vereen. They combed the area along Ocean Boulevard, the main highway through Garden City, and among the vacation houses, many already weatherized and closed for the winter. Widely circulated fliers with a photo of Ernie wearing a jacket and tie announced a $20,000 reward; the funds came from the office of Solicitor Jim Dunn ($10,000), from Horry County Council ($5,000 requested by Police Chief Gordon Harris) and from the Vereen family ($5,000). The reward would be worth about $60,000 today.

At first, the family hoped Ernie would be found alive. But as days passed into months, those hopes dimmed. The coastal area had stretches of undeveloped land, a harsh environment to search—black, gummy, shoe-sucking plough or "pluff" mud couldn't be crossed on foot; creeks and inlets rose and fell with the tide, creating an ever-changing landscape; dense, impenetrable brush still covered hundreds of acres along the coast. In November, Alan told reporter Norton something that he'd really appreciated during the ordeal: "There are still people out there beating the bushes…and there is still investigative work going on too," he said. "One thing I've tried to say hasn't found its way into print yet. And that has to do with how amazing and efficient all those FBI people and Horry County police are, and what amount of effort they've put forth. There were agents and police at the beginning who went forty-eight hours without sleep. It has been a tremendous effort—maybe more than we deserve."

Suspect Alvin Owens couldn't give them any guidance. He'd been admitted to Conway Hospital in a reported "hysterical coma" soon after his arrest. He said he couldn't remember anything about what happened; his trial was postponed so he could undergo a thirty-day psychiatric evaluation. He was found fit to stand trial, and his case was heard in January 1985.

Even without help from Alvin, a search of his home recovered his handwritten practice drafts of the ransom note and what he planned to say in the phone calls; his fingerprints were found on some of the documents. He'd also rented a portable Brother typewriter on October 6 and returned it on October 8, days before the ransom note was placed in Alan's mailbox; the typewriter rental details were on a receipt found in Alvin's house. Forensic examination indicated that the note was typed on a Brother or a Remington typewriter; tests showed it was "very possible" that the rented typewriter produced the ransom note.

Police also tracked down other evidence: Owens's son had Ernie's watch; Owens's daughter pawned one of Ernie's rings. While hair "matches" are no longer considered forensically sound, gray and white hairs consistent with Ernie's and different from Alvin's were found in the trunk of Alvin's car. On October 13, almost a month before the kidnapping, Alvin had arranged to buy a new car from a local dealer. He claimed he had a $200,000 insurance settlement coming that would pay for the car. Investigators found no evidence of a pending insurance settlement, and the sum corresponded closely with the amount demanded as ransom.

In his defense, Alvin claimed he had been forced against his will to participate. As indicated by the WUO signature on the ransom note, the Weather Underground, a left-leaning militant terrorist organization responsible for several bombings in the 1970s, had kidnapped Ernie and forced Alvin to type the note and pick up the ransom money. However, the Weather Underground hadn't been a presence in South Carolina, even before it began to fade from the national stage in the mid-1970s. That colorful but outdated claim didn't help Alvin.

Initially, Horry County solicitor Jim Dunn tried Alvin only for kidnapping. Ernie's body hadn't been located, despite all efforts. No one in South Carolina had ever been tried for murder without the victim's body. No-body cases had been tried elsewhere, but they were rare. And carefully selected. A solicitor gets only one attempt to win a criminal case; if a jury finds insufficient evidence and votes to acquit, the defendant can't be tried again. The double jeopardy protection in the U.S. Constitution forbids giving the state another stab at the defendant, even if the body or other important evidence is later found.

In a murder case, the body is key evidence. It establishes that the victim is deceased and the remains can indicate when, where and how he died—all important elements in a prosecution. Without a body, a defense attorney could argue that the defendant may have decided to disappear; why, he could even walk into the courtroom. Not all prosecutors are willing or able to risk the time and resources needed for a murder trial with no body.

In this case, those who saw Ernie Vereen regularly hadn't seen him after October 10. He was legally blind and suffered from angina, yet his eyeglasses and heart medication were left behind, along with signs of a struggle and a quick departure from his house.

Jim Dunn felt he had enough to prove a kidnapping: the typewriter rental, the similarity between the typewriter and the ransom note, the note claiming the writer was holding Ernie Vereen, the drafts of the ransom note at Alvin's house and Alvin's claim to the car salesman that he was soon expecting a $200,000 windfall.

On January 17, 1985, Alvin Owens received a life sentence for the kidnapping.

His attorneys appealed. They claimed the prosecution "made an excellent show for blackmail or extortion" but hadn't proven that a kidnapping occurred. In its opinion, the appellate court held that a case based on circumstantial evidence must have proof that points "conclusively to the guilt of the accused and must be absolutely inconsistent with any other reasonable hypothesis." A case requires a corpus delicti, which doesn't mean producing a physical body but instead means proving the elements of the crime. In this case, that the kidnapping had occurred was established by the circumstances of a struggle in Ernie Vereen's kitchen and "the fact that Mr. Vereen remained missing at the time of the trial." While no one saw Alvin kidnap Ernie, the evidence collected provided sufficient circumstantial evidence to connect him to the preparation of the ransom note.

The state supreme court upheld his conviction for kidnapping.

A year later, on January 3, 1986, the Horry County grand jury issued a murder indictment, alleging that Ernest Vereen was killed by "forcibly sedating him and/or roughening him up by violently manhandling him and beating him and/or depriving him of his life-sustaining medication and/or mortally injuring him by means or instruments unknown to the grand jurors." Because the murder occurred during a kidnapping—an aggravating circumstance—Alvin faced the death penalty.

During his twelve-year career as one of the Lowcountry's most colorful solicitors, Jim Dunn tried and won convictions in two other death-penalty cases: Rudolph Tyner, convicted of the 1978 killing of Bill and Myrtle Moon, and spree killer Rusty Woomer, who killed four and seriously maimed another in 1979. This would be solicitor Dunn's third death penalty case.

At trial, Alvin's attorney, public defender Ralph Wilson, questioned the quality of the police investigation and told the jury, "This case is riddled with doubts about what happened and when and where and how." In Jim Dunn's closing argument to the jury, he said, "I don't know where the body is. You don't know where the body is. Law enforcement doesn't know where the body is. But there's one man who knows where the body is....He has successfully hidden the body of Ernest Vereen....Is that the type of success we want to reward?"

The jury deliberated less than two hours before finding fifty-five-year-old Alvin Owens guilty of murder during a kidnapping, with a recommendation that the judge award the death penalty. The state supreme court affirmed.

Because Alvin Owens's lawyers made no closing arguments in the guilt phase of his May 1986 trial, a judge later ruled in a post-conviction relief hearing that he was entitled to a new trial.

In the period before the new trial, Ralph Wilson, one of Alvin's public defenders in the kidnapping trial, took the job of assistant solicitor with Jim Dunn. To avoid a conflict of interest, Dunn stepped down, and John Justice, a long-serving solicitor for Lancaster, Chester and Fairfield Counties, was appointed as special prosecutor in the case. Alvin was again convicted.

Alvin appealed that third conviction. His attorneys argued that a statement he made to fellow inmate Albert Burgess (that he "shot Mr. Vereen with a .22") shouldn't have been admitted because Albert Burgess was acting as Alvin's legal advisor at the time. Therefore, attorney-client privilege should apply. The court disagreed. The court held that inmates who serve as "jailhouse lawyers" can help prepare petitions and do research, but they aren't "professional advisers" protected by attorney-client privilege. Besides, Alvin had done plenty of talking to other inmates, making statements such as "they'll never charge me for murder, or convict me of murder because of where the body is, south of Myrtle Beach."

Alvin's attorneys also argued that a recent U.S. Supreme Court decision meant that evidence from his previous trial for kidnapping couldn't be used as an aggravating factor to try him again for capital murder. Ultimately, after his multiple appeals, his death penalty verdicts were set aside, but the state supreme court upheld his conviction for murder and his life sentence.

A month after Ernie disappeared and after Alvin was arrested, a couple related to Ernie by marriage talked to reporter John Norton, who wrote a lengthy recap of the case in *The State* newspaper. They'd lived at the park for several years and still felt safe there, even after the shock of having Ernie snatched from his home. People lived there, they said, even if they could afford something better because it was a secure, safe community where people tended to know each other.

In 1990, Alvin Owens wrote to Lesia Shannon, a reporter with the *Myrtle Beach Sun-News*, asking her to visit him while he was on death row. She hadn't covered his trials, but another inmate she had interviewed suggested Alvin get in touch with her. In her article, she wrote about her doubts about visiting the Broad River Correctional Institution in Columbia: What were the protocols? How would she know where to go? Why did he want to talk to her?

When they met, Alvin brought a "jam box" to tape-record their conversation, so she could take the recording with her. He talked about his family and gave her copies of his short stories and poems.

As they talked, a "very nice, short man" came around with a cooler and offered them soft drinks. They declined, but he insisted. She thought he must be a kindhearted visitor. No, the man insisting they needed something to drink was Pee Wee Gaskins, South Carolina's most prolific serial killer. Described as intelligent, outgoing and completely without empathy, Pee Wee initially went to prison in 1976, serving multiple life sentences for ten murders, though he admitted to more. He had earned the privileges of a prison trusty, which gave him the freedom of movement in 1982 to blow up death row inmate Rudolph Tyner with C-4 explosives. By coincidence, Tyner had been solicitor Jim Dunn's first death penalty case for the murder of Bill and Myrtle Moon in their small Murrells Inlet grocery store. The Moons' son grew tired of the years of Tyner's appeals and retrials, so he hired inmate Pee Wee to kill Tyner while he sat on death row. Killing Tyner on death row earned Pee Wee a trip to the electric chair, a sentence carried out less than a year after he gave reporter Lesia Shannon a Mountain Dew.

Broad River Correctional Institution houses South Carolina's death row inmates. *Courtesy of South Carolina Department of Corrections website.*

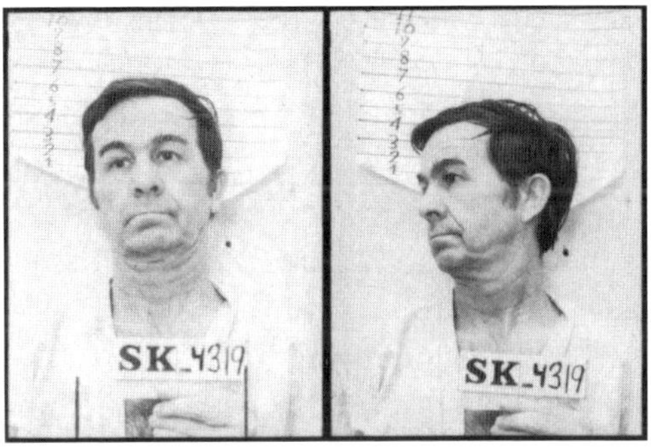

Pee Wee Gaskins's mug shot, taken at Central Prison. *Courtesy of Richland Library, Columbia, SC.*

(For more on Pee Wee Gaskins and his death-row murder, see *True Crime Stories of the South Carolina Midlands*.)

Throughout his trials, Alvin Owens told anyone who'd listen that he was innocent, that he'd been set up. In 1994, a decade after Ernie disappeared, Alvin's former defense attorney Ralph Wilson asked him if he'd be willing to lead investigators to Ernie Vereen's body. Despite spending six hours bulldozing a thirty-square-yard area near the U.S. 17 bypass in Myrtle Beach, no sign of remains was found.

Alvin Owens died in 2017.

OLDEST UNSOLVED MURDER?

Identifying what is truly the oldest unsolved murder in a region or a state is difficult. Sometimes unsolved cases just drift out of sight beneath the ever-growing stack of new crime reports over the decades. But a murder unsolved for more than one hundred years is certainly in the running for "oldest" and is likely to remain on the list given the apparent impossibility of solving it.

On September 22, 1908, twenty-four-year-old L. Pressley Reeves was killed, shot in the head with a single shotgun blast. According to one colorful version, just after dark, mules pulled a wagon loaded with cotton into the yard of the family's farm near Reevesville in Dorchester County, not far from modern-day Interstate 95. In the back lay L. Pressley Reeves with blood from his fatal wound staining the cotton in the wagon.

To help in the search, Governor Martin Frederick Ansel sent bloodhounds from the penitentiary by special train to follow the trail of the killer or killers.

Pressley Reeves was killed only three years after state game wardens began protecting fish and wildlife. *Courtesy of South Carolina Department of Natural Resources via Wikimedia Commons.*

At the inquest, the testimony of Pressley's father, A.M. Reeves, lacked the colorful detail of the earlier news account. The father said his son Pressley had left the farm to fetch two farmworkers from the field and take them about two miles down the road to their homes. The men had helped pick cotton that day. The father's testimony didn't mention bloodstained cotton in the wagon. He did say Pressley's body was slumped over the wagon's dashboard. He felt for a pulse, unharnessed the mules from the wagon and "followed the trail of the blood to the place where he was shot." He didn't know who'd shot his son, but he named a couple of local men who'd "kept picking at Pressley."

One witness testified he'd heard an unnamed witness say Pressley needed to be killed; another said he was a bully. Others were told to keep quiet and "we will get you out of it." A nearby neighbor, Eliza James, testified that she heard "scattering talk about somebody would kill Pressley Reeves. Never heard anybody say they would kill him." A.J. Hoover said he "never heard anyone making any threats," but he had "heard that something would happen."

More than one witness testified that somebody saw two men on a ditch bank at the time of the shooting. The mishmash of "he said" and "he contradicted" left no clear answers after the inquest.

The father was used to hearing threats of violence against his son. He knew it went with his son's job as one of the state's first game wardens. Young Pressley patrolled the woods, rivers and swamps of Dorchester, making sure hunters and fishermen obeyed the game laws—and that wouldn't make him popular.

A December editorial in *The State* newspaper argued in support of the new game regulation. Some said the laws hurt the poor who needed the fish and game to feed their families. But editorial writer James Henry Rice Jr.—noted conservationist and, later, the state's chief game warden—argued that the rich, the idle and the often out-of-state powerful hunting clubs and their lawyers were the ones taking the game and fish for pure sport. He pointed the finger at those who poached for profit, ridiculing the small amount they made while taking food from local families—citing one who'd made $45 (about $1,600 in today's dollars).

In his editorial, Rice also called out a known "fish pirate" for Pressley's murder. In bold type and all capital letters, he said, "Rather than lose the chance of making forty-five dollars in an unlawful business, a neighbor of Pressley Reeves murdered him, and today walks the road haunted by the ghost of the man he murdered and at night can not sleep, according to the testimony of his wife, because he sees Pressley Reeves looking at him through the window!" Rice claimed the Audubon Society knew the man's identity.

The pointed fingers, the contradictory stories, the slender threads of believable evidence, the certainty someone knew the killer—none of it ever resulted in a publicly released name or a conviction. In 2020, James Green, a Reeves great-grandson, was following the family law enforcement tradition and serving as an agent with the South Carolina State Law Enforcement Division. Drawing on his own experience in law enforcement and his knowledge of the close-knit, closed-mouth nature of the rural region, he told reporter Thomas Novelly, "There are still rumors about it floating around."

A Still Unsolved Case

Many police departments and sheriff's offices now have their cold case files posted on websites, with photos and abbreviated accounts and contact information for leads. The posts give the facts but don't try to convey the loss, questions and hope that surround each story. In the background of each case report stand family members, friends, investigators and a community who are all searching for answers.

As technology has improved, headlines frequently carry news of a long-cold case suddenly solved, decades after reason argued it would never happen. Solving a case believed to be hopeless can offer a glimmer to those families still waiting. But sometimes the answers stay stubbornly locked away.

On June 24, 1972, three young teenage boys were off on the kind of adventure lots of boys in the rural South likely enjoyed at one time or another—they were looking to steal some watermelons. Michael Akey, age fourteen, would be a freshman at Beaufort High School in the fall, but on this day, it was summer break, and he and his friends were reveling in their freedom.

On Highway 170, in front of the South Carolina Electric and Gas Company office, they caught a ride with a man driving a blue 1962 or 1963 four-door Chevrolet; he might have been a Marine. The man agreed to drive them to a watermelon field on Highway 40, and they reportedly enjoyed some beers he'd offered. Michael stayed in the car with the driver while his friends went to pick out the watermelons. Before they returned, though, the car drove away. And no one ever saw Michael Akey alive again.

Michael was described as five feet, six inches tall and weighed one hundred pounds. His hair was a tad on the long side. A photo showed sandy blond hair, a smile that said he wasn't quite comfortable in his coat and tie for picture day and ears he hadn't yet grown to fit. When he went missing, he was wearing red and white shorts with wide stripes and a yellow and blue T-shirt. Michael's friends described the driver of the Chevrolet as in his twenties with short hair but could offer nothing that helped find him or his car. At the time, a deputy sheriff said he thought Michael had probably run away from home.

Three months later, in mid-September, a one-hundred-dollar donation from an anonymous neighbor of the Akeys opened a reward fund, hoping that would generate leads. It didn't. The family learned nothing useful for almost six long years. When it came, the news was heartbreaking and inconclusive.

On February 8, 1978, while clearing land not far from the ruins of Whitehall Plantation on Lady's Island, workers uncovered a skeleton. Lady's Island is largely rural, but part of it sits within the Beaufort city limits. Forensics experts at the Medical University of South Carolina in Charleston could say only that the remains were the right age and size to be Michael Akey. The bones were laid to rest in the Beaufort National Cemetery. His obituary listed his parents, a brother and two sisters as his survivors.

Finding the body reignited the investigation. The remains offered no clues on the cause of death, but officials suspected foul play. After attending a homicide investigation course in Columbia, investigator Sergeant Bob Houston and medical doctor Charles B. Hanna from Spartanburg experimented with an unorthodox method of identifying skeletal remains. Using a photograph of Michael and a motion picture made of the skull, they were able to superimpose the images and match key points to make a reasonably reliable identification of Michael Akey.

Two decades later, in 1999, another investigator, Captain Bob Bromage, began taking a fresh look at Beaufort County's cold cases. His investigation of Michael's case prompted him to ask the county solicitor's office to petition for a court-ordered exhumation, though the detective wouldn't

The ruins of Whitehall on Lady's Island near Beaufort. *Courtesy of U.S. National Park Service.*

share with the press what, if any, new evidence the cold-case review had uncovered. Beaufort reporter Lori Yount described Michael's two sisters at the exhumation site, standing hand in hand as they watched the "battered, child-sized casket" raised from the grave in 2005.

In 1978, when his remains were initially found, the state crime lab could perform only rudimentary testing. By 2005, mitochondrial DNA testing, which identifies descendants through the mother's lineage, was routine. Mitochondrial DNA can be extracted from bone and hair, when tissue and fluids are not available for traditional DNA nucleus testing. Months later, the FBI lab in Quantico, Virginia, conclusively reported that the remains were Michael Akey, as the family had both assumed and feared for almost thirty years.

Knowing they'd found Michael provided some resolution, but the identity of the killer remains unknown.

A Con Man or a Companion?

The crime cases that make headlines in the Lowcountry sometimes began elsewhere and only came to an end in South Carolina. Such was the still-mysterious death of Daniel Sterling Tondevold on Fripp Island in 1985. Much about Tondevold is a mystery—or is it? Unraveling the relationship between someone dubbed "an international man of mystery" and a 1914 Knoxville, Tennessee debutante was difficult because of the many interwoven strands and unanswered questions.

The preservation of most crime stories requires at least one person curious enough to dig out and capture the details. For this case, Damion Moore began what he called tedious research to find the facts behind an episode of *Unsolved Mysteries* that initially aired on December 4, 1991. "Tedious" research because, in early 2002, government documents, newspapers and genealogy records weren't a simple mouse click away. But, as he explained in a 2018 post on his *American Crime Journal* website, Damion found hundreds of like-minded, dedicated researchers who made information available to one another in online chats. As Damion said, "Nobody had a digital footprint in the early aughts." But researching a man named Tondevold was easier than finding a Smith or a Jones.

Damion also cautioned that the "Unexplained Death" segments on *Unsolved Mysteries* weren't as bound by facts as the program's segments attempting to track fugitives who'd committed crimes. The "unexplained" segments weren't initiated by law enforcement who provided investigative details but rather by families looking for answers. The "Lady and the Tramp" episode raised intriguing questions, and Damion Moore went searching for the answers.

The mystery of Dan Tondevold—the "tramp" in the segment's title—was linked with the very public life of "the lady," debutante Ellen McClung, a direct descendant of James White and James McClung, among Knoxville's founding fathers. At age thirty-four, Ellen married Thomas Berry. Was he really a coal tycoon from Rome, Georgia? That mystery appeared early in the tale, since little is known about Thomas. The couple had a son four years later, when Ellen was thirty-eight—not an easy age to birth a first child. But young Hugh Lawson McClung didn't hamper his parents' socialite, jet-setting lifestyles. He was sent away to elite schools and came home only for holidays and breaks. Ellen and Thomas restored several historic Knoxville-area homes and actively participated in managing charities. Ellen had studied in Europe and held a master's degree when few women were so well educated.

Fairfax or Riverview in Tennessee, built in 1840, was one of the homes restored by Thomas Berry and Ellen McClung. In 1977, they built a smaller home, Berrymount. *Courtesy of Brian Stansberry via Wikimedia Commons.*

When Hugh turned eighteen, in 1951, the second mysterious element appeared in the story. Hugh, reportedly angry that he was being disinherited, shot his grandmother and his father with birdshot from a .410 shotgun while the family vacationed in West Palm Beach, Florida. The six-foot, two-inch teenager then went on the run, after taking a shot at a patrolman at the West Palm Beach Country Club.

Hugh's father recovered from his injuries, but his grandmother died a few days after the shooting. When Hugh was captured, his wealthy parents arranged—with help from doctors and the county sheriff—to have him evaluated. His mother was convinced his actions resulted from a head injury when he was fifteen. He was diagnosed with dementia praecox—now known as schizophrenia—and admitted to a private asylum in Chicago, where his public story ends. He was later released from the asylum and, in 1963, died of pneumonia in Mexico at age thirty-one.

In Knoxville, Thomas and Ellen continued to live their elegant, engaged lives, eventually settling into a hilltop home they named Berrymount where they planned to spend their retirement. The loss of her son caused Ellen heartache over the years, especially after Thomas died in 1978 and she moved into her later years alone.

Soon after Thomas's death, Dan Tondevold came to Berrymount to visit Ellen. They told people they'd been corresponding for fifteen years and that Tondevold was her godson. Or that he was a friend of Hugh's. The stories changed and the facts remained unclear. Some of her friends and employees thought Dan looked like Hugh and maybe was filling a void for her.

Dan Tondevold had worked as director of merchandise for the I. Magnin luxury clothing chain and was responsible for opening the first United States–based retail store in Japan, bringing American retail culture to postwar Japan. For almost two years, Tondevold, who was bilingual and well-traveled, worked in Japan, acquainting himself with the culture, laws, traditions and business environment. Following World War II, rebuilding the Japanese economy and the country's economic partnerships was an important U.S. initiative.

In 1978, he moved into the Berrymont estate's guesthouse so he could work on a book he was writing, and his friendship with Ellen grew until, four years after he'd arrived, she gave him power of attorney to manage her affairs. Two years later, in 1984—the year she turned ninety—he proposed a long visit to Charleston, South Carolina, where the winter would be warmer.

At the end of March 1985, after four months in Charleston, Ellen was to fly back home to Tennessee with her aide, and Dan would drive her Mercedes and bring along her furs and jewelry. When she walked into Berrymount, she found the house dark, the utilities disconnected. Dan had used the power of attorney over Ellen's affairs to obtain a mortgage on her home. A bank foreclosure was pending on her beloved Berrymount—and she had no money in any of her accounts. Equally disturbing, Dan Tondevold hadn't returned as arranged with her car, her furs or her jewelry. He was reportedly still using her credit cards to fund his stay at an expensive resort on Fripp Island, a small barrier island between Charleston and Hilton Head.

According to the *Knoxville News-Sentinel*, Ellen took out a warrant charging Dan Tondevold for fraudulent breach of trust, though the "warrant does not specify how much money was taken nor give the value of the antiques."

The day the desk clerk told Dan that his cards were maxed out and he needed to present a new means of payment, Dan walked out of the resort hotel, leaving behind a suicide note in his suite.

His body lay in a remote swampy marshland on Fripp Island and wasn't discovered until two weeks later. He'd apparently shot himself in the head with a vintage gun taken from Ellen Berry's house. His only forms of

One of the local residents enjoys the sun along a Fripp Island waterway. *Courtesy of carlfbagge via Flickr.*

identification were Ellen's credit cards. The only person available to identify the decomposed remains was a security guard from the resort, even though he hadn't known Dan Tondevold all that well. The body was cremated, as his suicide note had requested.

Then a new set of mysteries arose. Was the body Dan Tondevold? Or was it a substitute he'd found to disguise his escape? Dan had advertised for a chauffeur in the Charleston paper's want ads before the twosome left Berrymount for their trip. Why did they need to hire a chauffeur-houseman as they returned to Tennessee? Had Dan and the chauffeur run off together? Or was some poor jobseeker the substitute body found on Fripp Island? Did Dan place the ad to search for a replacement companion for Ellen? Did he steal her money? Or did he remain as her companion until the funds she had to support her lifestyle eventually ran dry? Maybe he didn't want to tell her the truth about the state of her affairs.

The *Unsolved Mysteries* episode was memorable for many viewers. It suggested that Dan Tondevold had shown up out of the blue at Berrymount, perhaps planning to con a lonely, elderly woman of her fortune. But Damion Moore's careful research uncovered a photograph of Ellen and her husband, Thomas, with Dan Tondevold at the 1968 Ladies Hermitage Association Fall Outing, a group that raised funds to maintain President Andrew Jackson's home near Nashville. So Ellen knew Dan at least ten years before Thomas died. Their relationship wasn't a hit-and-run con job but a long-standing friendship. He served as her companion for seven years. Dan Tondevold was apparently successful, socially and financially secure in his own right for at least part of his life.

Interestingly, Damion Moore's research (and apparently the background research for the *Unsolved Mysteries* episode) failed to find financial records indicating any fraud or records to indicate what Dan Tondevold's own financial situation was during this period. In his younger years, he'd lived a lavish lifestyle with an older and very successful male companion, and he'd worked as a top executive and knowledgeable spokesman for a cutting-edge retail company. As the United States sought to build a better economic relationship with Japan, Dan was someone who could offer insight and answer questions. But Dan's sexual orientation had reportedly led to a long-lasting schism with his parents.

As a young man, Dan went from being an honors student at Las Vegas High School, active in several clubs and leadership positions in 1951, to an arrest for extorting $1,200 from a Las Vegas bakery owner. In 1954, the twenty-year-old threatened to write letters that "would ruin the bakery operator," according to police records and the *Reno-Gazette Journal*. He was arrested as he walked out of the bakery after picking up an envelope "filled with some money and scraps of paper." He would only say he needed money and "consistently declined" to explain why he targeted the baker, since neither claimed to know the other. Dan pleaded guilty to attempted extortion and, as an unusual condition of probation, was sent to a mental hospital for treatment.

Damion Moore points out that, in the 1950s, homosexuality was classified as a mental disorder in the American Psychiatric Association's manual. For those expecting Dan to be a con man living off a naïve older woman, his police record was evidence of a criminal past. But it could also be evidence of a young man living without family support and desperate for cash. A few years after his brush with the law, Dan was living in San Francisco in a very public gay relationship with a wealthy man. By 1973, he was on the team introducing I. Magnin's Tokyo business ventures.

In 1985, Ellen was left almost destitute, living mostly on annuity payments arranged as part of a large gift she and her husband had made to the University of Tennessee. She left Berrymont and moved to an apartment in Jefferson City, Tennessee, until her death at age ninety-eight in 1992.

A portrait of the elegant, redhaired young Ellen McClung is in the collection of the Knoxville Museum of Art. The details of what really happened are still uncertain.

7
FAMILY CONNECTIONS

The Bigham Family

Some families leave legacies of public service, integrity and leadership. Other leave legacies of anger, avarice and entitlement. Some are the nightmares you hope never to find yourself married into. Do evil legacies linger longer than the good? Or are tales of misdeeds and murder just more interesting?

Stories about the Bighams have circled around the small town of Pamplico and the Great Pee Dee River region for more than one hundred years, leaving an indelible mark on the crime history of Lowcountry South Carolina.

The Bigham family was among the original settlers in the area, arriving before the Revolutionary War. They farmed great stretches of the rich black soil and became known as men not to cross. Their influence could, it seemed, protect them from paying the price for their cruelty and crimes, even murder.

This PeeDee branch of the Bigham family tree starts in the late 1800s with Leonard Bigham, when he bought more than two thousand acres on the west side of the Great Pee Dee River. He was also building a reputation as a vengeful bully who would turn violent with those who crossed him. He'd shot one of his farm workers because the laborer and his wife defied him one day and refused to leave their sick children alone to continue working the fields. When Leonard was tried for the murder, the jury found him not guilty. The victim's widow didn't back down, though. The night he killed her husband on the front porch of their cabin, he'd also shot her in the leg. She brought charges against Leonard for assault—and won. He was sentenced to three months in jail and fined fifty dollars but avoided jail thanks to testimonials that he was too old and feeble to serve time. Even when Leonard lost, he still managed to win.

In 1887, Leonard's son, Leonard Smiley Bigham Jr., was elected as the first state senator to represent Florence County after it was divided from Marion County. When Senator Smiley Bigham died in January 1906, plenty of rumors surrounded his death—rumors so consistent that they must have contained the seed of truth. The only questions that the community as well as the family mused about were exactly what poison his wife, Dora, had used and whether she'd slipped into his milk or his coffee. Widow Dora would cryptically respond to her family's jests: "The old fool is dead, isn't he?"

Years later, author Katharine Boling married into the Boling family, who farmed the land once owned by the Bigham clan. Her husband's great-grandfather had been brave enough to testify against one of Leonard Bigham's descendants—and he'd slumped over dead on the

A Pee Dee rice barn dating to the late 1800s. *Courtesy of Brian Bill, U.S. Fish and Wildlife Service via Wikimedia Commons.*

witness stand during the trial. Katharine's fascination with and research into the Bigham family saga became the 1972 book *A Piece of the Fox's Hide*. Most of what we know about the Bigham family murders and trials is thanks to journalists who covered the trials and to Boling's research (with help from her husband and seven children). The threads are long and tangled, but she pulled them apart.

After Senator Smiley's mysterious death, the senator's son Smiley III followed in the footsteps of his grandfather, the original Leonard Smiley Bigham. Smiley III was indicted for killing a young boy who worked for the family, chasing him, pushing him down and driving a nail into his ear. His trial was set for October 1909.

In September, the month before the trial, Smiley III's brother Dr. G. Cleveland Bigham was visiting the Avant family's beach house at Murrells Inlet with his wife, Ruth, when another tragedy struck. In the dim light of evening, Dr. Bigham managed to trick an inebriated William Avant into believing that the woman in the pale dress on the beach was a decoy for robbers or maybe even a ghost. Avant fired at the wispy figure and killed Dr. Bigham's wife, Ruth.

Rumors—those shadowy reports that often come close to the truth—said that Dr. Cleveland Bigham instigated the murder of his wife to keep her from testifying at his brother Smiley's trial. In the Bigham family, blood was tainted and thicker than anything, and Ruth wasn't blood kin. They hadn't trusted what she'd say on the witness stand.

In Ruth's death, charges were brought only after out-of-town witnesses came forward to say they were fishing nearby at the time of the shooting, and given the lighting and the distance, the shooter must have clearly seen that it was a woman. Cleveland Bigham and William Avant were convicted of the reduced charge of manslaughter, rather than murder.

Cleveland received a three-year sentence and paid a bond that allowed him freedom until the appellate court heard his appeal. When the court upheld his verdict, he left South Carolina to avoid being rearrested and sent to prison. Law enforcement published a description of the fugitive: "twenty-eight years of age, full round face, reddened as if by dissipation, auburn hair, light brown eyes, countenance full and open, but showing capacity for strong and merciless acts."

His friend William Avant also fled, heading to Texas, but was captured and returned to serve his sentence. Cleveland Bigham stayed on the run even though the bond his family posted put the Bigham property at risk of forfeiture if he didn't return.

The tales of vicious tragedy among the Bighams had only begun. Over a decade after Smiley III's trial, in 1921, widowed Dora was living in the Bigham homeplace with her sons Edmund and Smiley III and daughter Marjorie McCrackin and Marjorie's two children, Dora's grandchildren. On January 15, Edmund summoned aid, saying he'd come home and found everyone—his mother, brother, sister, niece and nephew—shot. His mother had enough breath left to tell him that his brother Smiley had shot everyone. He found Smiley in the woods, dead of a gunshot wound, a pistol in his hand.

That was Edmund's version of the massacre but not the version supported by the scene. Edmund was arrested for the murders.

As Edmund sat in jail awaiting trial, his wife was arrested and sent to a county jail cell of her own—for trying to smuggle a vial of chloroform to her husband. According to Kingstree's *County Record*, she asked for help from one of the other inmates who worked inside as a trusty "whose confidence Bigham supposed he had obtained." He hadn't. The trusty handed the chloroform over to the jail authorities, and she was promptly arrested. As it turned out, they'd been on alert for some underhanded activity because they'd been privy to the notes Edmund had been sending to his wife through another inmate. Physicians who inspected the drug said it was enough to kill.

Mrs. Bigham, as newspapers identified her, didn't spend long in jail, and Edmund's March 1921 trial for murdering his entire family began as scheduled. He was sentenced to death. The appellate court later overturned the verdict and granted him a new trial. Three years later, his second trial was held in the Horry County Courthouse in Conway. Word had spread about the gothic tragedy of the Bighams—but few people in distant Horry County felt afraid of the family—so the courthouse was packed. The "circus," as Edmund called it, did not disappoint.

This was the trial where Katharine Boling's husband's great-grandfather George Steele had the courage to testify against Edmund and died of a heart attack while in the witness box. As Steele was pronounced dead, in Katharine Boling's account, Edmund issued his own proclamation:

"Edmund was on his feet, hurling words at them all: 'You see! You see! God is punishing those who malign and persecute me. Those who tell their lies against me are dying, don't you see? *God will cut you all down like flies!*'"

That wasn't the only unusual moment at the trial. A flood of biblical proportions inundated Conway. Two lawyers punched it out in the courtroom at one point. Dora Bigham's skull, with a distinct bullet hole, was introduced as a prime exhibit in an attempt to shock a confession from her son. In the end, the outcomes of his first trial were repeated: a death sentence, an overturned verdict, an order for yet another new trial.

After two death sentences and six years spent facing charges in court, Edmund Bigham finally decided, before his third trial heard its first witness, to plead guilty in exchange for a life sentence. Edmund served over thirty years in prison until 1960, when Ralph Gasque, the state senator serving Marion County, arranged for Edmund's parole into his custody. Edmund died two years later in Marion at the age of seventy-seven. Dora Bigham's skull sat in a hatbox in the Horry County property room until Florence's state senator Tom Smith reclaimed it. It was buried in a Pamplico cemetery in 1990.

Soon after Edmund's 1927 guilty plea, J.A. Zeigler, editor of the *Florence Morning News-Review*, published his account of the multiple trials, and his book remained the definitive resource until 1972, when Katharine Boling's book offered the broader perspective provided by the passage of time.

As Katharine Boling asked questions and researched the murders fifty years after the events, she found people in the rural farming communities still reluctant to talk about the Bighams. Their vicious shadow remained long and menacing. Without her work, though, the convoluted details of the story would have disappeared, making it easy to forget the evil legacy of one family dynasty.

Fate and Family

Starting in June 2021, with the double murder of a mother and son, the little-known stretch of cypress swamps and hunting preserves between Charleston and Hilton Head made headlines worldwide. To understand the swirling mysteries around the murders, those unfamiliar with the South and, more particularly, the swampy regions of Hampton and Colleton Counties, needed lessons on how to pronounce Alex ("Ellick") and Murdaugh ("Murdock"), the chief suspect, and on the history of his "powerful family dynasty."

What was missed in most of the coverage by those who flew in and tried to take the measure of an insular, generations-old society were the subtleties. "Power" was often interpreted as "fear" or "threat," rather than as favors bestowed or kindnesses acknowledged. To outsiders, a culture of hunting meant violence and uncontrolled testosterone rather than the need to feed a family or to protect land and crops from deer overpopulation or from roving feral hogs.

Those from the South, especially those in small towns or rural areas, understand that favors and slights are remembered, sometimes for generations. Kindness and consideration can build bridges. Politicians aren't seen only on election-year billboards but also at church and in the grocery store or sitting on their front porches.

The mystery of who shot and killed Maggie Murdaugh and her twenty-two-year-old son, Paul, with two high-powered hunting rifles near the dog kennels on their 1,700-acre hunting estate opened up an unseen and little-understood world. And after the judge's gavel clapped down for the last time and the television satellite trucks pulled out of town, some of the mysteries remained, still unresolved or misinterpreted.

True, the Murdaugh family had an unusual dynasty—four generations had served in the solicitor's office (an old term for district attorneys or prosecutors still used in South Carolina) for almost one hundred years, passing the elected office from father to son. Often overlooked, though, was that solicitors are elected. And people must like or respect the candidates and the job they're doing. Otherwise, they'll elect someone else. Maybe in some jurisdictions, mob-style force coerces voters, corrupts elections and cements dynasties with threats and violence. In the case of the Murdaughs and the position of solicitor for the Fourteenth Judicial Circuit, none of that was ever alleged. Rather than force, they used favor—which tends to last longer and leave a better taste in people's mouths. And keeps people coming to the ballot box.

The family names are confusing because, as with many Southern families, names and nicknames are handed down. The first Murdaugh solicitor was Randolph Sr., who served from 1920 until his death in 1940. Randolph Sr. spent twenty years in elected office and, at the same time, built a successful private law practice and what eventually became one of the most influential law firms in the state. Not until 1976 did the state make the position of solicitor a full-time job and forbid any private practice. Handling personal injury cases in civil court paid better than a government job as a prosecutor. But a prosecutor has the power to decide what cases are brought to criminal court and how severe the possible penalties—and which charges are dismissed or never pursued. On both civil and criminal sides of the court, Randolph Sr. built a foundation for the lawyers who would follow in his family.

Randolph Sr. wasn't afraid to prosecute cases that others would find difficult or unpopular. He went after child molesters, including a minister, and law enforcement officers who killed without justification. Randolph prosecuted a federal Prohibition agent who raided a man's boat, shot him and then claimed he had immunity as a federal agent. Not in Randolph's eyes, he didn't. In another case, Randolph Sr. took three years to investigate the murder of a Yemassee doctor's wife, who died in the couple's bedroom in 1934 of "knife and hammer wounds." Initially, the coroner's jury found she'd died by suicide after she stabbed her husband in the head, he said, because he couldn't sing a gospel song she requested. Randolph Sr. wasn't satisfied with that explanation or with the suicide claim. Two years later, in news coverage of another case, the reporter noted that "Solicitor Murdaugh was late arriving due to his having been detained at Yemassee investigating a case there." It took two trials, but Randolph Sr. eventually convicted the doctor of manslaughter in the death of his wife.

To avoid a difficult footnote to his story, most accounts of Randolph Sr.'s death simply report that he died suddenly. On the night of July 18, 1940, Randolph Sr. sat in his car, flashing its headlights on a street crossing near the train tracks that ran through Hampton County. The conductor saw him and couldn't figure out if the driver was sending a message. The lights just flashed regularly, on and off. As the train neared, the car pulled onto the tracks. The conductor blew the horn and tried to brake, though he had no space to stop. In the train's light, he could see the driver waving his hand. And laughing.

The second prosecutor in the family was Randolph Jr., better known as Buster. Already a successful trial lawyer in the family firm, he was appointed to serve his father's term in 1940 and was continually reelected until 1986, when he reached the state's mandatory retirement age of seventy-two.

According to author Jason Ryan, a judge early in Randolph Sr.'s career called him "one of the hardest working, cleanest, and most capable solicitors in the entire state." His son Buster set a different tone. For starters, he filed suit against the railroad company for his father's death, despite the deliberateness of Randolph Sr.'s actions; CSX railroad settled rather than fight it in court.

Unlike his more courtly, hardworking father, Buster was a glad-hander and back-slapper, famous for the cookouts to which he invited law enforcement, judges, attorneys and others from around the state. He was master of the courtroom. His delivery style could be dramatic and theatrical; he sometimes reenacted death scenes during trial, with himself playing either the victim or the killer in front of the jury. He could control a courtroom, and he was always well-prepared and personally invested in his cases. He won most of the time. Buster sent nineteen men to death row.

As did his dad before him, he worked with legendary Beaufort County Sheriff Ed McTeer (see chapter 8). In a 1943 case, they worked together on a crime that crossed county lines and were able to get a Black man who'd been wrongly convicted of rape off death row and eventually exonerated.

No prosecutor can bring every possible case to a jury trial. No office has the staff or the resources or the courtroom space to prosecute everything. Decisions must be made. Buster knew that dropping a case or making sure it received a lighter treatment could be an easy benefit to a potential defendant, a favor that might set someone on the right track or might accrue dividends for the prosecutor in future goodwill. When people speak of the Murdaugh family's power, Buster most often wielded the power of judicious beneficence.

Not that Buster didn't have a temper or a taste for retribution when someone played him wrong. Journalist Jason Ryan quoted one of Buster's lawyer friends: "He was just as loyal to his enemies as he was to his friends." And as with the movie stereotypes of Southern sheriffs—or, in this case, Southern prosecutors—decades of successful reelections breed a certain confidence, a sense of entitlement, of noblesse oblige and the reciprocal expectation of gratitude. Buster made good money from the civil cases he brought, and he had a reputation for never turning away a poor person who needed help. His role as solicitor kept his name in people's minds and, in turn, brought business to the law firm he built.

Like many prosecutors, sheriffs and corporate CEOs in positions for long periods of time, Buster developed a sense of invincibility. In 1956, he faced federal indictments for his participation—some say as the mastermind—in a bootlegging ring selling untaxed whiskey. Much of the evidence against the defendants came from a federal agent who'd gone undercover as a sheriff's deputy. Seventeen men, including the Colleton County sheriff, were convicted in federal court in Charleston. Buster's attorneys argued that the scathing testimony about his favors to the criminals was nothing more than calculated revenge on him for his good work as a crime fighter. Buster and two others were found not guilty. One month after the jury acquitted him, Buster was reelected to another term as solicitor.

In 1970, with his political control in that section of South Carolina solidified, Buster met Pat Conroy, a young teacher destined to be the region's iconic best-selling novelist. Conroy famously was fired as teacher at a small school on Beaufort County's Daufuskie Island because the school board didn't approve of his teaching methods. After he argued his own case to the court about why he should be reinstated, the not-yet-famous writer met the "cock of the walk in this part of South Carolina" solicitor, who "sat in the jury box and laughed his ass off at several things I said," as Conroy later wrote. He recorded their first meeting in his book *The Death of Santini*:

> *"Boy, you really know how to put on a show. You scared the living hell out of those bastards. But you're going to lose your ass."*
>
> *"What if I'd had you as a lawyer?"*
>
> *"You'd be teaching in that little school of yours tomorrow morning. But you ain't going to be teaching ever again."*

Then Buster offered to send Conroy to law school: "Then you come back and work for me. I'll make you the goddamnedest lawyer you've ever seen."

The Hampton County Courthouse was built in 1878. *Courtesy of Upstateherd via Wikimedia Commons.*

As captured by one of the South's finest writers—one who, as Jack Ryan pointed out, knew how to recognize a character—that vignette paints a vivid picture of Buster Murdaugh at the height of his powers.

Despite the criminal charges he'd faced, his growing sense of command and his sometimes-crude language and behavior, Buster was elected to serve the five counties of Allendale, Hampton, Jasper, Walterboro and Beaufort as solicitor for forty-six years. He continued to practice civil law at Peters, Murdaugh, Parker, Eltzroth & Detrick (known as PMPED), the firm he helped build. A few months after his wife died in 1997, Buster too passed away at the age of eighty-three.

The governor appointed Buster's son Randolph Murdaugh III, called Randy, to fill the solicitor's seat. Randy was also successful in a courtroom but not as aggressive as his father. Times had changed, and that good ol' boy demeanor wasn't as effective in front of juries increasingly filled with folks who'd moved in from elsewhere. Public opinion also had cooled on most death penalty prosecutions.

Randy had learned from all the years he worked with his dad and watched him perform in a courtroom. Randy was gentle and more approachable than his father. While his courtroom presence was more restrained, he had learned the importance of visual demonstrations. He would have the doctor who performed autopsies on the county's homicide victims come out of the witness box and, with a red marker, draw the victim's bullet wounds on Randy's white dress shirt. He wore the red-stained shirt in front of the jury for the rest of that day's session.

As the caseload for circuit solicitors continued to grow, Randy supported the state's pretrial intervention program. Jason Ryan cited one case where, at Christmas each year, a former defendant thanked Randy for giving him a second chance. "'To be a good solicitor,' said Randy, 'you have to develop the insight and be able to recognize when you can help a person and keep him a productive person in society.'"

Not all acts of mercy were rewarded with a life turned around, however. In April 1990, Henry Louis Wallace, a young man from Barnwell, was charged with the attempted rape of a sixteen-year-old Barnwell girl. The attack took place in Allendale County, under the purview of Fourteenth Circuit Solicitor Randy Murdaugh. Because Henry, a former naval weapons tech on the USS *Nimitz*, was deemed a first-time, nonviolent offender, the solicitor put Henry into the pretrial intervention program. Unknown to investigators, to the solicitor or in the records reviewed for the pretrial "catch and release" program, the body of Henry Louis

Wallace's first murder victim had just been pulled from in a pond in Barnwell.

Thanks to the intervention program, Wallace moved to Charlotte, North Carolina, in 1991, with no record of violent crime. He quickly became the most prolific serial killer in the city's history. Counting victim Tashanda Bethea in Barnwell, he killed eleven women before he was captured in March 1994. (For more on Wallace, see *Charlotte True Crime Stories*.)

Prosecutors must make decisions about how to handle cases, which ones to pursue and which can't be convincingly presented to a jury. Not every murder is prosecuted with the vigor of a *Dateline* episode. In 2005, just before Randy resigned after almost twenty years as solicitor, he explained to journalist John Monk why a 2001 arsenic poisoning death of a Columbia businessman vacationing in Hilton Head hadn't been prosecuted. The victim's wife had been arrested and charged but later released on bail. Monk had questions about why the case wasn't moving. "Because it is circumstantial and scientific, it is an awful lot more difficult case to try than it is where you got a video of somebody shooting somebody during an armed robbery," said Randy.

In June 2009, eight years after the poisoning death, Duffie Stone—one of Randy Murdaugh's assistant solicitors who'd been appointed to fill his term when he retired—entered a *nolle prosequi* or "nol pros," notifying the court that the solicitor's office would not pursue the poisoning case.

The last Murdaugh associated with the solicitor's office never actually served as the solicitor. Alex Murdaugh was appointed by his father, Randy, as a "volunteer deputy solicitor" and given a badge. But he never took an oath of office and worked on only a few cases.

Alex loved his grandfather Buster and spent a lot of time with him. Whether by nurture or nature, the grandson had his granddad's personality—boisterous, a bit of a bully, a drinker and a glad-hander. Alex developed his own reputation for always smiling, always remembering names, helping people out, inviting them to the continuation of the Murdaughs' famous cookouts and hunting parties for judges and others in law enforcement. Unknown to his friends and colleagues, Alex also developed an opioid addiction and had trouble matching his income with his lifestyle.

Eventually—though not automatically—Alex was hired by the large, successful firm that bore his family name. Representing injured plaintiffs in court paid better than the solicitor's office, especially in Hampton County, one of the highest verdict jurisdictions in the nation. South Carolina

The Colleton County Courthouse, built in 1823, is in Walterboro. *Courtesy of Upstateherd via Wikimedia Commons.*

allowed lawyers to shop for the best venue in which to try a case, provided the defendants had some connection to the county chosen. Largely thanks to the work of the PMPED law firm, Hampton County juries responded generously to injured plaintiffs suing large corporations, and Alex won some big verdicts starting in 2012. In a two-year period, his share of verdicts or settlements was over $7 million.

Alex lacked the courtroom flair of his granddad or the diligent preparation of his great-granddad. But he was amiable and outgoing, convincing when talking to clients, lawyers or judges. Rather than risk a trial, big cases are often settled. And Alex was an effective rainmaker for the firm, bringing in high-potential cases.

But not all years were lucrative, and his spending outstripped his income. He began a complicated shell game of borrowing from law partners and friends, borrowing illegally from his clients' trust accounts, getting unsecured loans from a local bank owned by longtime family friends and eventually setting up a complicated system of stealing from clients through a fake settlement firm he named to sound like a legitimate settlement broker.

In 2019, the house of cards began to tumble when his son Paul was involved in a boat crash where one young woman was killed and other passengers injured. Lawyers suing for the injured and their families figured Alex Murdaugh, the boat owner, had money, and they were demanding to see his financial records. Those document requests threatened to reveal all that had been hidden.

The details of the night Alex's wife, Maggie, and their son Paul were killed filled international newscasts, newspaper headlines, podcasts and TV documentaries. His jailhouse phone calls were replayed on the *Murdaugh Murders* podcast, and his trial in the Colleton County Courthouse for their murders was broadcast live on television. In the criminal trial that started on January 25, 2023, he was sentenced to two life sentences plus the additional state time he faced for his financial crimes. He pleaded guilty in federal court to financial fraud and conspiracy and was sentenced to a forty-year federal term, to be served along with his state sentences. Despite pleading guilty to a lengthy list of other crimes, he continued to deny that he hurt or killed his wife and son.

8
THE LAW

McTeer, the High Sheriff

Among South Carolina law enforcement figures, few have earned as many nicknames as Beaufort County Sheriff J.E. "Ed" McTeer. He took office in February 1926—the youngest sheriff in the United States, at the age of twenty-two—appointed by the governor after his father's unexpected death from pneumonia. Over the years, Sheriff Ed McTeer was known as the boy sheriff, the sheriff without a gun and the white witch doctor.

In a place where people turned to root doctors to solve personal as well as physical problems and where many were raised to fear "black" or dangerous root medicine, it was a wise sheriff who made sure he understood what many white residents in the region ridiculed or ignored. The overlapping cultures of white and Black, rural and city, farms and businesses, newcomers and those born on the land, all required a lawman sensitive to subtleties and differences.

Much of his official job as sheriff dealt with the usual family squabbles and drunken disputes that continue to fill police blotters. But in the 1920s, Beaufort County and the surrounding region also dealt with moonshiners and gangsters as well as with root medicine—its practitioners and customers alike. In his own words, McTeer's memoir tells of his respect for the history and culture that enslaved people brought from Africa and the Caribbean islands. He recognized the influence of a root doctor as akin to that of a priest, and he respected that power.

McTeer asked questions, learned from those who practiced root medicine and recognized how making use of what people believed could help him solve cases or heal fractures in the community.

Almost fifty years after he took office, the retired sheriff penned his memoir, *High Sheriff of the Low Country*, and opened the book with a testimonial from Dr. Eagle, a well-known root doctor. Dr. Eagle attested that he and the sheriff had "worked closely together helping people who were in trouble and under the influence of Spells or needed help from Mystic Powers." Long after his last term as sheriff, he continued his work as a white witch doctor, or what he called "a poor man's psychiatrist," from the back room of his real estate office.

Early in his career, Sheriff McTeer got to know Dr. Eagle's predecessor, the region's iconic Dr. Buzzard (born Stepheney Robinson) and eventually worked with and learned from him. Clients often hired Dr. Buzzard to help when they faced a court trial. He would sit in the courtroom wearing purple or green sunglasses that made his eyes invisible and "chew the root" on the judge, on the solicitor and on McTeer, as sheriff. The root-chewing was to "render the evidence harmless and provide the best outcome for the accused," McTeer explained in his memoir.

Solicitor Randolph Murdaugh Sr., the first in the Murdaugh family line of solicitors (see chapter 7), asked the sheriff about the packets he kept finding in the courtroom, "little packages of things on my desk, like the leg of a chicken and some dirt and feathers and things." The solicitor kept throwing them away, but more appeared. The sheriff explained that someone was "trying to put a spell on you…to keep you from convicting the person." For Solicitor Murdaugh, that helped explain why some of his witnesses would suddenly refuse to testify against defendants in criminal cases.

The day Sheriff McTeer came early to the courtroom and saw Dr. Buzzard in his sunglasses sitting in the back and a white powder sprinkled on the sheriff's desk and on the solicitor's and judge's desks, he called the doctor aside. "Stepheney, I don't mind you chewing the root on me; I don't care if you chew your teeth down to your gums. But next time you put root powder on our desks, the judge will 'root' you with a sentence of about 60 days." Dr. Buzzard grinned and promised to bring him two nice chickens, signaling an understanding. Times changed, and years later, Dr. Eagle, who'd assumed the mantle at Dr. Buzzard's passing, said he didn't go to court and chew the root anymore; trials took too much waiting. He just sold the root and told the client to chew it for himself.

The Beaufort County Courthouse was built in 1883. *Courtesy of Luther's Pharmacy and The Albertype Co., Brooklyn, via Wikimedia Commons.*

While root doctors played on people's subconscious susceptibility to suggestion, not all worked safely for their clients' benefit. During World War II, a significant number of the region's young Black men were being rejected from the military draft because of irregular heartbeats. According to a *True Magazine* account reported by author Baynard Woods, two men heading for their military physicals at Columbia's Fort Jackson died en route on the bus and others became ill. The draftees confessed to buying a potion to keep them from being drafted. The FBI contacted Sheriff McTeer, who tracked the vials to an elderly, illiterate man who'd bestowed on himself the title Dr. Bug, root doctor, and begun a lucrative business selling potions. The FBI lab analysis showed that Dr. Bug was selling small vials of moonshine mixed with lead arsenate (an insecticide containing lead and arsenic), a poison that caused heart irregularities. The real magic in the case was that Dr. Bug hadn't killed more of them.

According to Sheriff McTeer, Dr. Bug was convicted of administering poison, marking the end of his career as a root doctor. Baynard Woods said the federal court charge was, more specifically, practicing medicine without a license. (Selling roots or spells was allowed, but not selling potions or ointments that were used on or in the human body.) Rather than a year in prison, Dr. Bug agreed to pay a $1,000 fine. An IRS agent stopped Peter

Murray, aka Dr. Bug, as he left the courtroom and got another $2,000 from him for back taxes.

McTeer's pragmatic approach to law enforcement helped when an uptight state governor wanted him to put a quick end to a social experiment on Cat Island. A health and nature fanatic, who also managed a New York magazine conglomerate that included *True Detective* and *True Romance* magazines, chose the South Carolina coast for a utopian back-to-nature health retreat. He bought Cat Island, across the creek from Beaufort, for $12,000 and set about building Sea Island Sanctuary.

Word that the resort was a nudist camp stirred all kind of interest. The state's stiff-necked governor wanted the immoral bunch of them arrested. The locals were curious. McTeer sent deputies on a "fishing trip" to find out what was going on, but they turned their boats toward the mainland and left when a group of nudists—who'd been alerted they were coming—ran out on the beach to welcome them.

McTeer saw no harm in the visitors and residents doing whatever they wanted without their clothes on, as long as they were on their own property. He "delayed" action against the group until the political scrutiny died down. The sheriff's approach worked. The demise of the Sea Island Sanctuary was certainly foreseeable, according to the sheriff: "the stalwart and at times ferocious Beaufort County mosquitoes, red bugs and sand gnats took their toll on the nudists' tender and exposed skins when spring arrived and accomplished what the strong arm of the law had failed to do." The nudist colony closed with no fanfare.

Not all cases ended with a wry smile. Some were deadly serious. In one case, a white woman accused a Black man of raping her. The alleged attack had occurred in neighboring Jasper County, but the attacker had run for shelter to Beaufort County, Sheriff McTeer's jurisdiction. In questioning the man, the sheriff believed the fugitive's alibi witnesses and his account of what happened, that he hadn't committed the crime. But the Jasper County sheriff didn't see it that way and made the arrest.

During the trial, the woman's husband tried to physically attack the defendant, vowing to kill him. The wife melted into hysterics. McTeer knew the outcome was inevitable, despite his misgivings about the validity of her claim. The defendant was convicted and sentenced to death in 1943.

As his execution date drew near, Solicitor Buster Murdaugh—Randolph Sr.'s son—contacted McTeer to ask if he believed the man guilty or innocent.

"'Solicitor,' I said, 'an innocent man will die if you don't stop that execution. I'm as guilty of raping her as he is.'"

Solicitor Murdaugh convinced the governor to commute the sentence to life in prison. Two years later, in 1945, the same woman accused another man of raping her. Solicitor Murdaugh wasn't going to be party to another miscarriage of justice. Under questioning, she finally admitted that she'd lied in both cases because she couldn't convince her husband that they should move out of the rural Lowcountry. Psychiatric evaluation found her to be unstable.

The wrongly convicted man was released and paid compensation by the state. "But," wrote McTeer, "no amount of money could ever eradicate the horrors that he must have endured, awaiting the executioner on death row. And it all happened just because a woman wanted to change her place of residence."

Dealing with mentally unbalanced people was part of a sheriff's charge, then as now. A call came that a man in the Sheldon community had gone crazy. His neighbors had him barricaded inside a house, threatening him with sticks if he tried to come out. As the crowd continued to grow and as the officers failed to calm him down, McTeer asked around about the man and learned he liked sweet rolls. In fact, he had a genuine passion for them.

McTeer had a bag of his favorite sweet rolls delivered to the scene, waved the bag around so the Sheldon man could see it through the window, took a roll out and began eating it with obvious relish. That got the man to talking and eventually drew him out of the house and into the police car. At first, McTeer lured him with a whole roll. Then he had to break them in half as they drove toward the jail, then fourths, then single bites. They barely got him in the cell before he realized the rolls were gone and he turned violent again. McTeer later said that stretch of road always reminded him of "where I got so many miles to the sweet roll."

Rarely does a rural sheriff's work involve solving a whodunnit. But Ed McTeer proved his abilities even with puzzle mysteries. He felt he'd inherited "the sight" from this mother. Or maybe his careful attention to those in his jurisdiction and his intuition about how people behave got the credit, but he solved cases—even when prosecutors or juries might not see things as he did. In February 1949, William Moseley Swain Jr. was found dead at the bottom of the basement steps in his elegant plantation home, Belfair. As author Baynard Woods described the times, in the period following the Civil War, northern wealth flowed south to buy up destitute plantations for use as private hunting grounds or retreats. For some, Bluffton became the "North's nuthouse," as northern families sent certain family members south for safekeeping on these estates.

The coroner thought the scene at Swain's Belfair looked as expected: an accidental fall down the stairs onto a concrete floor. The examining doctor found a small gash on Billy Swain's head and "an eight-inch fracture of the skull." The coroner's jury, as they stood over the body on the basement floor, found the cause of death undetermined. Sheriff McTeer didn't agree.

Following a lead, McTeer went to see Victor Strojney, a transplanted northern engineer now raising cattle on his Beaufort County property. Victor explained that he'd seen Billy Swain outside the bank in town the day before. Billy had just borrowed $11,000 from the bank, and he repaid Victor $100 he owed him and loaned him $600 from the money he'd just borrowed from the bank.

That sounded convoluted to the sheriff. Why repay money and, at the same time, loan money to the one you'd borrowed money from?

The two friends had returned from town to Belfair and shared several drinks. Billy went upstairs to bed. As Victor was letting himself out, he heard a noise and found Billy at the bottom of the basement stairs. Why, wondered Sheriff McTeer, was the guest leaving after the host had gone to bed? McTeer had the whiskey glass found lying next to Billy tested—and discovered Victor's fingerprints. McTeer arrested Victor Strojney and charged him with murder.

Victor hired a good lawyer—one who had lobbied for McTeer's appointment to replace his father as sheriff back in 1926. He demonstrated other ways Billy Swain could have gotten the wounds on his head, and the jury acquitted Victor. Good detective work may not always win before a jury.

But others were justifiably impressed with McTeer's skills of observation and detection, including Solicitor Murdaugh. The two were called to the scene where a Mr. Wilson, who maintained a post office in his country store, had been viciously beaten and stabbed repeatedly. McTeer found pieces of a .22 rifle with blood and strands of Wilson's hair on the stock. The scene suggested that the gun had jammed and then broken when it was used as a club. He sent men to search for the missing barrel, describing the direction where they'd likely find it. Judging from the account books, about $1,000 of post office money was missing, not counting whatever had been in the store till.

McTeer told the solicitor he knew who'd done it. "Ed," Solicitor Buster Murdaugh said, "you know the county and your people, but I don't think this one can be solved without leaving the store."

But the sheriff knew that two unemployed brothers who were often up to no good lived nearby. Tracks from the store came and went from the direction of their house. As he predicted, the rifle barrel was found in the woods to the left of their tracks, just the direction a right-handed man would sling it away. A gun and an icepick were missing from their mother's house. Rather than credit Sheriff McTeer's observational skills and attention to detail, some preferred to think he had otherworldly powers.

McTeer noted that his rookie years as sheriff were spent busting stills and capturing moonshine shipments. He wrote about stakeouts in the swamp, with mosquitos eating him alive, twigs poking him in sensitive spots and bootleggers more than willing to shoot first and figure out who was spying on them later.

Eventually, times changed in Beaufort as elsewhere. A sheriff can't please every voter. Some didn't like that he ran a real estate business while serving as sheriff. Some didn't like his stance on race issues, on one side or the other. After years of running unopposed, he lost his last hotly contested election in 1962. But Ed McTeer wasn't a man who sat on his porch and rocked. He continued to sell real estate and promote the region to visitors. He continued to help people solve their problems as a "poor man's psychiatrist," and he wrote four memoirs of his life as sheriff and of the Beaufort region. He died on December 28, 1979, at the age of seventy-six, after serving a record-setting thirty-seven years as sheriff.

MELVIN PURVIS

Melvin Purvis, one of the FBI's most famous agents, was born in Timmonsville, South Carolina, about ten miles from Florence. Even growing up in his small town, Melvin felt he was destined for something big—though his phenomenal accomplishments during the FBI's 1930s war on gangsters were not always acknowledged by the FBI. A personal animosity developed between him and his onetime advocate, the powerful but jealous J. Edgar Hoover.

Melvin Purvis didn't set out to be a lawman of any stripe. He got a law degree from the University of South Carolina in 1925 and practiced law in Florence for a couple of years at P.A. Willcox's firm. His dream job, though, was in the Foreign Service. With no openings there, he instead applied and was accepted into the FBI in February 1927. The agency had suffered scandals and a rough start as the nation's law enforcer; the FBI's new director, J. Edgar Hoover, vowed to redeem the agency and set its future course.

During Melvin's first three years with the bureau, Hoover heard good things about the energetic, capable new agent, so he assigned the twenty-seven-year-old as the agency's youngest field office chief. In the next two years, Melvin held postings as special agent in charge (the highest-ranking agent in an assigned region) in Cincinnati; Washington, D.C.; Oklahoma City; and Birmingham before Hoover sent him to Chicago, which was rife with crime during the raging 1930s.

Chicago was where Melvin became a household word as a crimefighting G-man. According to his nephew, writing about his uncle almost eighty years later, Melvin set an FBI record in 1934 that still stands. In a four-month period, he captured more "public enemies" (now listed as the FBI's Most Wanted) than any FBI agent before or since: John Dillinger in July 1934, followed by Pretty Boy Floyd and Baby Face Nelson in separate raids in November 1934.

Melvin was quick to point out that those captures were all team efforts, not him acting along. He was described as a handsome, soft-spoken Southern gentleman. At five feet, seven inches tall and a slender 130

The Biograph Theater in Chicago, where Melvin Purvis and the FBI shot Public Enemy No. 1 John Dillinger in 1934. *Courtesy of Stephen Hogan via Wikimedia Commons.*

pounds, he wasn't imposing, but he was always well-dressed, charming and hardworking. His agency secretary in Chicago said, "Many of us had crushes on him then."

John Dillinger's death outside Chicago's Biograph Theater on July 22, 1934, captured America's attention. Every detail of the story was reported, from the mysterious lady in red who aided the FBI to details about Dillinger's criminal career. He robbed banks and even a few police stations, he survived shootouts, he twice escaped from jails—once with a wooden gun, not a gun carved from soap, as told in later tales. He became a celebrity bad boy with a reputation as a Robin Hood, likely as exaggerated as his other exploits. But with his celebrity as "America's Public Enemy Number One," he represented a growing lawlessness and viciousness among 1930s era gangsters with names still famous today: Ma Barker and her boys, Creepy Al Karpis, Bonnie and Clyde, Pretty Boy Floyd, Al Capone and Machine Gun Kelly. While their stories captured headlines during the grim days of the Great Depression and some cheered on their exploits, the gangster crime wave was beginning to hit regular people where they lived. Dillinger's death marked a turning point, both in the roundup of the gangsters and in the public's relief that they could rely on law enforcement to keep them safe.

That had been one of J. Edgar Hoover's avowed goals, to fight bad guys. But Hoover, even with the power of his vision, could also be thin-skinned and vindictive. Melvin Purvis became a media darling. He was kind, generous about his teammates' contributions, handsome and personable, as well as deadly effective and in the right place at the right time. Hoover became jealous, and his vendetta against Melvin—aptly made the title of the book by Melvin Purvis's son Alton—continued even after Melvin's death.

In 1935, a year after his record-setting captures, Melvin resigned from the FBI. He moved to Lombard Street in San Francisco and went back to practicing law. He gave product endorsements for Dodge cars and for breakfast cereal, complete with badges for the Junior G-men Corps in boxes of Post Toasties. That was soon followed by a stint as host of the Junior G-man radio show and its club membership of 260,000. As a Hollywood technical advisor, he became friends with Clark Gable and almost married Janice Jarrett, the model known as the Lucky Strike Girl, but he apparently got cold feet and the wedding didn't happen. He headed to Europe, where, in 1935, he had an interesting wild boar hunting excursion with Hermann Göring, commander of Hitler's Luftwaffe and creator of the Nazi Gestapo. Melvin Purvis had a fan in Göring, it turned out. According to Melvin's nephew, Göring greeted him at his Berlin hotel with "Hallo, beeg G-man." The two met again during the Nuremberg trials after World War II, when Melvin served as deputy director of the War Crimes Office and Göring stood trial. Drawing on his investigative background, Melvin had returned to Germany as part of the investigation into Adolf Hitler's suicide.

Photo of FBI Agent Melvin Purvis in 1934. *Courtesy of Scoop Archive via Wikimedia Commons.*

Melvin's list of activities after his short but illustrious FBI career indicate a man searching for his second act. He'd been a headliner in 1930s national crimefighting, but what could he do next to top that? Where could he direct his intelligence, energy and ambition?

He wrote his autobiography, published in 1936. In it, the self-effacing man portrayed himself as a team player, not one to grandstand: "I am not a gunfighter. I am not a wily sleuth. To tell the truth I was thoroughly frightened every time it fell to my lot to carry a gun on a foray of any kind." He wrote how much he admired those "who never knew the emotion of fear…those joyous daredevils." But he was on the scene because "only the knowledge that there was a job to do kept me functioning."

Purvis's marriage is often reduced to a single line in biographical sketches, but his son Alston, in his book about his father and J. Edgar, gave an endearing account of his parents' longtime love affair. Rosanne Willcox's attorney father had died at the age of fifty-six, just four years before Melvin was hired by the Willcox firm as a newly minted lawyer in 1925. When Rosanne attended Winthrop College in Rock Hill, Melvin would drive from Florence to take her on dates. Those who knew the couple believed that, from the early days of their courtship, she was the love of his life. But Rosanne's mother apparently didn't consider young Melvin a suitable catch for her daughter. The early death of Rosanne's father had left Marie Willcox having to sell their horses, their home in Florence, their private rail car and their mountain house in Saluda, North Carolina. Marie built a smaller house on Cherokee Road and went to work at the Florence Public Library. She knew her daughter's life would be easier if she married well, and Melvin Purvis from tiny Timmonsville didn't look like a man with position or good prospects.

Melvin left Florence in 1927. The couple didn't discuss or record the status of their romance at the time, but in 1931, Rosanne married a Standard Oil executive. Alston Purvis reported that her bridesmaids cried during the wedding—and not for joy.

In the spring of 1938, Melvin was in Florence and visiting friends who lived on Cherokee Road. By good fortune, Rosanne was visiting the house at the same time. They hadn't seen each other for about a decade. Rather quickly, she divorced her husband, and a month later, the couple married on September 14, 1938, in the First Baptist Church in Charlotte. They built a house on Cherokee Road in Florence, patterned after a Natchez, Mississippi mansion they admired, and had three sons. Melvin soon left to serve during World War II and earned the rank of colonel.

After the war and his work with the War Crimes Office, he returned home and continued his search for fulfilling employment. He bought the local Florence radio station and worked on some federal law enforcement reviews and projects at the behest of former South Carolina governor and then-senator Olin Johnston.

Built in 1925, the old Florence Public Library is on the National Register of Historic Places. *Courtesy of Robert Thomas McKenzie Jr. via Wikimedia Commons.*

On February 29, 1960, Melvin Purvis died at his home in Florence of a self-inflicted gunshot wound from the .45 automatic pistol presented to him by his fellow agents when he resigned. The FBI pronounced it a suicide, and Hoover didn't send a condolence letter to the family. A later investigation found that Melvin was trying to remove a tracer bullet lodged in the gun when it accidentally fired. He was fifty-six years old and survived by his wife and three sons.

Reuben Greenberg

Among Lowcountry South Carolina's colorful lawmen, Reuben Greenberg stands out for a variety of reasons. Hired by Charleston's long-serving mayor Joe Riley as chief of police in 1982, Chief Greenberg came into a city struggling with crime and racial tensions that threatened its attractiveness to tourists. Greenberg billed himself as the only Black Jewish police chief in the nation. The description wasn't what made him stand out, though. His actions did. He was known as a hands-on cop: he'd show up on crime or accident scenes, he'd direct traffic, he patrolled the streets on horseback or wearing roller skates and he popped onto the police radio in the middle of the night. He spoke his mind, often attracting criticism. And he made the popular tourist town safe during a period where most U.S. cities saw dramatic increases in violent and drug-related crimes.

He could be tough on his officers, but they knew he worked hard and expected them to do no less. Word spread when the roller-skating chief arrested a bicycle thief one Saturday and again when he arrested a robbery-assault suspect at 5:00 a.m. He explained the early-morning capture to journalist Barry Seigel: "I learned where he was staying and wanted to visit him when he was sleeping.…Besides, it's fun going on those calls. Better than sitting behind a desk."

In February 1983, soon after he was hired in Charleston, Chief Greenberg made news by sticking up for one of his officers. The patrol officer crashed his cruiser three times in seven months, at a cost to the department of $5,680 (about $18,000 today). He's "an excellent officer," said the chief, "and once he gets to the scene, he does a very good job." Providing him with a chauffeur to get him to the scene wasn't an option, so the chief assigned him to the city's horse patrol. In October 1983, the *Los Angeles Times* recounted that story in a front-page feature article about the chief, with a photograph of him in a short-sleeved shirt and roller skates talking to a patrol officer in a car.

Interviews, formal testimonials and Facebook posts show the continued respect his officers had for him because of his loyalty to them.

His crime solutions were bold but common sense. Foot patrol shouldn't be used as punishment, he said; put the best officers on the street where they're visible. Hire young officers and put them in running shoes—he called them the Flying Squad—because most street criminals are young and quick to run. Assign an officer to attend every parole hearing in Columbia for locals convicted of burglary or violent crimes; that resulted in 93 percent of felons from Charleston serving longer sentences and not coming home to make trouble. Pay attention to the things that encourage crime: make public housing safe by conducting criminal background checks on residents; monitor school truancy; help the homeless population with food, safe shelters and medical care; closely patrol the street corners where drugs are sold. Recognize that police officers hate paperwork and require that they file a written report for any use of force or for pulling a gun. Pay attention to small things: when robberies at local ATMs ticked up, he partnered with a local bank to place an ATM in the lobby of the police station so people had a safe, well-lighted place that was always open to withdraw money late at night—and an easy way to get cash to pay fines, as a bonus.

He knew the value of visibility for his officers—and for himself. Five years after this son of a Black mother and a Russian Jewish father born in Texas came to Charleston, he and the city faced what was often a powder keg situation for civic leaders. The Ku Klux Klan sought a permit to march in downtown Charleston. The Rosen Hagood Law Firm's online commemoration of the chief's career said he supported granting the parade permit, as was the group's constitutional right. But the permit was granted for two o'clock on an August afternoon—never a cool or comfortable time to wear robes in the heat and humidity of Charleston. And Chief Greenberg said he would lead the group "to keep them safe." Looking back on that event, Mayor Joe Riley said, "This is what you had: a brilliant, black, Jewish police chief leading a Klan march."

When Hurricane Hugo ravaged Charleston and the surrounding region on the night of September 21, 1989, Mayor Riley—who served in that post for forty years, before he stepped down in 2016—and Chief of Police Reuben Greenberg, along with others, provided important leadership. The Category 4 winds and the storm surge from Charleston Harbor devastated the peninsula and cut off utilities and key services for weeks. The chief, in his customary get-attention fashion, told his officers, "Don't arrest anybody. Beat 'em. We have nowhere to put them." Years later, a Facebook comment on the South Carolina Law Enforcement Officers Hall of Fame page remembered him telling officers, when dealing with looters, "Don't shoot 'em, but mark them real well." Even in crisis, he knew a colorful comment would grab attention—and get his message across.

At heart, Greenberg was a teacher and academic. One accomplishment that made him most proud was requiring that new hires have four-year college degrees—he graduated from the FBI Academy and held a degree from San Francisco State University and two graduate degrees from Cal-Berkeley. He taught at colleges and spoke at conferences and civic events around the country, talking about what became known as community policing and the need for police to be a visible and active presence without answering violence with bullying or retaliation. In 1989, he published *Let's Take Back Our Streets*, detailing his approach to engaged, successful policing designed to reduce crime and provide safety and stability.

Charleston's municipal building at 180 Lockwood Drive was named in his honor. After a series of strokes forced his retirement at age sixty-one, he settled on a mountainside in Tryon, North Carolina, where he delivered meals to elderly residents, frequented the local hot dog vendor and where almost no one knew he'd been one of the nation's top cops. He died on September 24, 2014, at age seventy-one, and was buried in Mt. Pleasant, back in the Lowcountry he'd served for twenty-three years.

9

SIDE TRIPS, CRIME BITS AND ODDITIES

The Lizard Man of Scape Ore Swamp

No one wants to be caught with a flat tire at two-thirty in the morning on a lonely rural road surrounded by swamp. But on June 29, 1988, that's where seventeen-year-old Christopher Davis found himself, in the dark, climbing out of the driver's seat to retrieve the jack from the trunk to change his tire. He was on his way home through Scape Ore Swamp after his late shift at McDonald's in Camden.

Without warning, from the trees and shadows near the Elmore butterbean shed and the artesian well, he saw a creature. Scaly, green and wet. Seven feet tall on its hind legs, three fingers with black fingernails on each hand. And glowing red eyes. Christopher leaped back into his 1976 Celica. The creature was standing right outside the driver's window. It jumped onto the car's roof, fell as Chris drove off, caught up with him and landed on the roof again, giving Chris a chance to study its long fingernails gripping the top of the windshield. Neither Chris nor his parents immediately reported the incident—the scratches and broken mirror on the car proved something had happened, but it was just too weird.

However, a few weeks later in July, a family living on the edge of Scape Ore Swamp called Sheriff Liston Truesdale, who dutifully listened as they described their Ford LTD being "chewed up" by something while it sat in their yard. That description downplayed the damage to the car, which, according to journalist Alicia Lutz, included "bite marks on the fender well, the chrome trim pulled off, the wheel well torn off and the wires chewed up and left in a chaotic bundle."

When Chris Davis and his father heard about that incident, they decided to see Sheriff Liston Truesdale. Because Chris had actually seen the creature, his account was the one that captured the headlines and the public imagination.

So began the summer of Lizard Man mania.

Christopher had been reluctant to tell Sheriff Truesdale what had happened. A creature clinging to the car's roof as he swerved back and forth to shake it off? The story was crazy, but the sheriff knew Chris's dad and found Chris believable. And Chris passed a lie detector test.

Sketch of Lizard Man by Charlotte artist Loyd Dillon. *Courtesy of Loyd Dillon.*

Other residents soon came forward reporting their own sightings of a red-eyed, seven-foot-tall monster. They couldn't easily admit to such weird stories, so they'd hesitated to come forward until others confessed to seeing the creature. Sheriff Truesdale said, "I probably collected ten names, and not one of them had reported it. No one came and volunteered information. I had to pull it out of them."

Who in their right mind would claim they saw a swamp thing? But the sheriff heard from people who'd heard someone else talk about seeing it, so he tracked down the sources and visited them to ask about their encounters. One man had stopped in the wee morning hours to get some water from the artesian well when he saw what he first thought was the silhouette of a dead tree, but then he watched a huge creature with red eyes move away into the swamp.

Reporter Randy Burns with Sumter's *The Item* newspaper told College of Charleston writer Alicia Lutz that "if it weren't for Liston Truesdale, I doubt you would have ever heard of the Lizard Man. Not because he promoted it, but because he didn't joke about it." He took the reports seriously, knew the people who'd seen something were scared, and he investigated.

With one reported sighting as early as the spring of 1986, Truesdale uncovered a total of three encounters before Chris Davis's sighting.

Word spread around Bishopville and Browntown. As recounted by Alicia Lutz, Emory Bedenbaugh, who owned the local radio station WAGS-AM, talked about the reports on his newscast and forwarded the story to Associated Press. Sumter's *The Item* published the drawing Christopher made for Sheriff Truesdale. Within days, civic boosters in Lee County saw value in letting outsiders know about the Lizard Man. "Browntown looked like a Carolina-Clemson game. It was bumper-to-bumper traffic," said Sheriff Truesdale. From Charlotte to Los Angeles, from *People* magazine to *Good Morning America*, national and international media picked up the story. Who could resist?

From the beginning, a mix of good fun, serious questions and some fear surrounded the stories. A Sumter car dealership advertised Lizard Man Discounts and Specials and offered samples of Swamp Juice, "the official drink of the Lizard Man." An area gun shop posted a $5,000 reward—but the Lizard Man had to be alive. A Columbia radio station offered $1 million for a capture—also alive. The station manager told the Sumter *Item*, "If this is real, we'd put it in a cage and charge people a quarter each to look at it, and I'm sure we'd make the money back." (An anticipated four million viewers? People were curious, but that might have been ambitious.) Sheriff Truesdale told author Lutz, "It was a mess. There were people walking around in outfits made out of chrome to try to entice the Lizard Man, because—you know—they heard he liked chrome. Other people were covering all the chrome on their cars with masking tape. I was scared some fool would get shot."

Those who'd been afraid to report what they'd seen were emboldened to come forward. Events began to escalate: trees were broken and crushed; metal drums carried from a dump, battered and thrown in the road; tracks led into the swamp. To follow the tracks, the SLED bloodhounds arrived from Columbia—but something deep in the woods turned back the dogs, and they wouldn't continue tracking. "Something in there scared them," Sheriff Truesdale said. "Whatever this thing was, it was scaring everyone who saw it."

The sheriff remained calm and professional, treating every report with the respect he'd give to any constituent who brought him a problem or concern. But he also warned that false reports would be punished as such. And he told the media to quit trying to make a joke out of it. The media had created this mania, and if they wanted to "make us look like Barney, you're going to jail."

Sightings eventually dwindled away, as did talk of the Lizard Man, until 1990, when the creature reappeared in two encounters: a passerby spotted him, and another had to swerve to avoid him in the road near the Elmore butterbean shed. Again in 2008, a minivan suffered a chewed-up fender with the Lizard Man's characteristic bite marks in the metal around the grill. A family who'd moved to town from New Jersey left soon after they learned that cats, a dog and a cow were found dead. Other reports came in about crunched metal and bite marks over the years.

In 2009, Chris Davis, age thirty-seven, was shot and killed at his home, and two young men were arrested in a suspected drug-related murder. News headlines identified him as "the man who claimed to see the Lizard Man," though he'd spent twenty years trying to move past that.

In 2015, a group from the College of Charleston mounted a multidisciplinary study of the Lizard Man. Their journey to Scape Ore Swamp was reported by journalist Alicia Lutz. The team's lizard expert was Dr. Eric McElroy, with a doctorate in ecology and evolutionary biology. "Some of my colleagues think I'm crazy to be doing this trip," he said. "I do want to see what kind of biology is being put behind this whole Lizard Man thing."

History professor Scott Poole joined as the group's expert on South Carolina history and on the folklore of monsters. He explained his interest: "As a monster historian, I'm interested in what *meaning* the people of Lee County have prescribed to the Lizard Man, if any at all."

Communication professor Robert Westerfelhaus, an expert in pop culture, wanted to explore the cultural and social practices and the commercial enterprises that grew up around the Lizard Man sightings.

The group commandeered a party bus owned by a College of Charleston alum. The *Hoobu*, a decommissioned school bus taking its name from the remaining letters after the S, C, L and S wore off, carried the group to Lee County. When the bus rolled into Bishopville, one of the welcoming party said, "I thought they were coming from Charleston and they'd be dignified! These people look like hippies!"

Dr. McElroy, the lizard expert, explained that a flashlight can make an alligator's eyes look red. Some lizards do run on their back legs, and some monitor lizards can stand as tall as five feet. But lizards are usually out during the day, not roaming around at night. And McElroy wouldn't expect a lizard "to go into the road and inspect a person changing their tire. That's just not something I would equate with typical monitor behavior."

Judge Bill Baskin, who served as municipal judge for thirty-seven years and loved Lee County history, rode with the research team to Elmore's butterbean shed. He explained that someone had stolen Elmore's air-conditioning equipment, used in the shed to dry the harvested beans. Lucious "Brother" Elmore had decided to stake out the shed to try to catch the thieves on the same night that Christopher Davis had his encounter.

Hearing a car stop on the road, Brother Elmore went to investigate, thinking he might've caught his man. He stood where he could look down on the road. He saw Christopher turn, scream and take off in a mad rush. He said the scratches and dings on the car were because the tire jack was still attached. And taillights reflected in his eyeglasses could look like glowing red eyes. The story was ready-made to scare people away from the butterbean shed, so one of younger Elmores made up some giant wooden feet and traipsed around in the swamp, and the deputies and sightseers started patrolling the road, scaring the thieves away.

That was the judge's story, reportedly as told by Brother Elmore. But the research team found that the sightlines weren't as described, that Elmore couldn't have seen Chris Davis's car that night from where he said he was standing.

Following other lines of inquiry, the team used kayaks and plenty of insect repellent to explore further back into the mud and vegetation of the blackwater swamp. Though Dr. McElroy donned waders and ventured farther than the rest of the team, no one spotted even a simple lizard, much less any signs of a seven-foot-tall part man/part lizard.

Dr. Poole explained that, particularly as newcomers settled in remote areas, it was "hard not to find a period in American history where there wasn't an interest in things in the woods, things in the swamps, things in the oceans." People are always fascinated and a bit fearful of "what lies outside of the campfire, what's just beyond the boundary of what we know about."

Some in Lee County felt that they let an economic boon slip away, that they missed the opportunity to have a popular festival like the one honoring the flying Mothman's 1966 appearance in Point Pleasant, West Virginia. Some resented being the butt of jokes and ridicule and didn't enjoy the curious crowds. Journalist Randy Burns summed it up: "There may have been a time when the community embraced the publicity, but now it's in the same category as the trash dump and the jail."

The South Carolina Cotton Museum, just off Main Street in Bishopville, houses the artifacts from the Lizard Man's heyday: plaster casts taken of Lizard Man footprints, photos of the cars damaged by its rampages, costumes and memorabilia from celebrations of Lizardmania. Country singer Jim Nesbitt, a Bishopville native, wrote an ode to the Lizard Man:

If you want to get yourself a little thrill,
take a little trip to Bishopville—

For a listen, check out "Jim Nesbitt Lizard Man" on YouTube. The gift shop sells T-shirts and hats, and a Lizard Man Stomp Festival was held in June 2024.

Moonshine and Hell Hole Swamp

In a region where swamps and wetlands are common, a place called Hell Hole Swamp must be something special. The boundaries of the swamp, now confined in the Francis Marion National Forest, run west from Jamestown toward Moncks Corner and north from Awendaw toward St. Stephen, mostly in Berkeley County. Hell Hole Swamp moonshiners reportedly cooked more illegal corn liquor than anywhere else in the state. Its closest rival was Upstate South Carolina, but in the mountains, illegal operations shifted easily back and forth over the border with North Carolina to avoid revenuers and weren't confined to South Carolina. And the mountains didn't offer the lucratively thirsty market that Hell Hole bootleggers found in Charleston's Prohibition-era blind tigers.

For anyone who tries to penetrate its mucky, thick undergrowth and sluggish waterways, "Hell Hole" may seem an obvious name for the place. The name was recorded on a 1773 map of the Charleston area drafted by James Cook for the British as tensions grew prior to the Revolutionary War. During the war, Patriot General Francis Marion, known as the Swamp Fox,

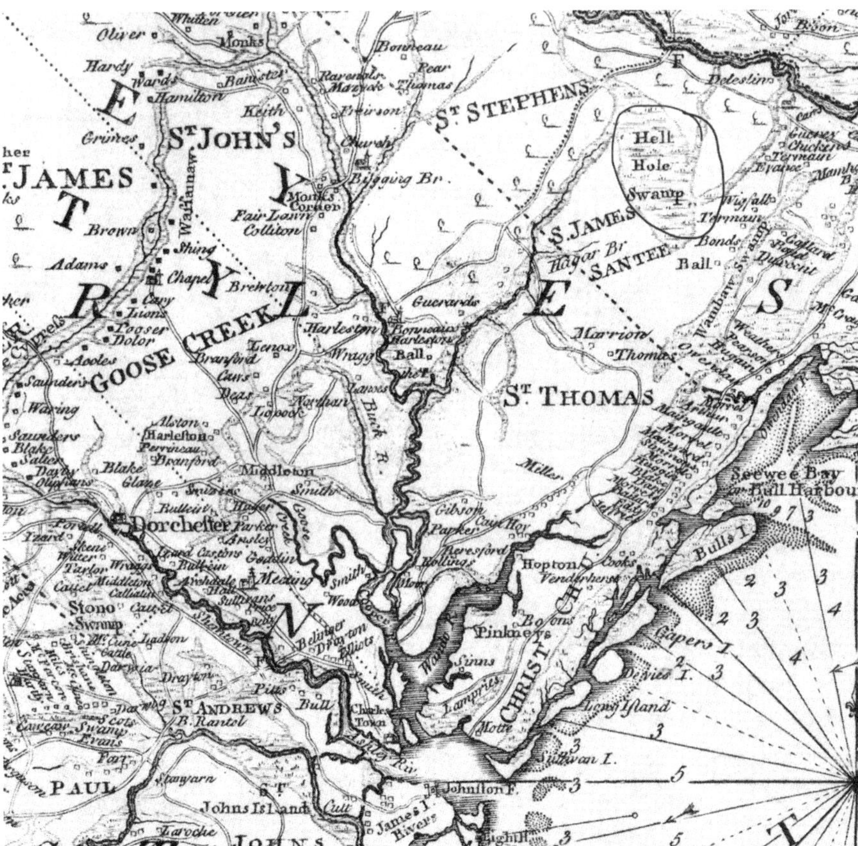

Excerpt of James Cook's 1773 map of the Charleston area showing Hell Hole Swamp. *Courtesy of David Rumsey via Wikimedia Commons.*

mounted raids on the British soldiers, using his knowledge of the swamps to appear and disappear. According to legend, British General Cornwallis wrote King George about how their attackers vanished into "one hell of a hole of a swamp."

Moonshine was a common craft in the rural South long before Prohibition began in 1920. Transporting corn in the form of distilled corn liquor was easier than transporting the crop itself over long distances—the liquor didn't rot in transit and the money to be made was better. Starting in the late 1700s, as a means of replenishing the federal treasuries depleted by the Revolutionary War, the taxes on legal liquor continued to grow. As any economist knows, taxing what people are going to buy no matter the price doesn't hurt demand—but it felt as if they were taking profits that should go to the still owners. In reaction, bootleggers in Hell Hole Swamp and in the Southern Appalachian Mountains turned tax avoidance into an art form.

Illegal, cash-based businesses inevitably create warring elements, which earned the county its "Bloody Berkeley" nickname. Hell Hole Swamp hid plenty of illegal stills and plenty of people with rivalries and reasons to fight and plot against each other. They didn't like competitors. Even more, they held a deep animosity for federal agents or revenuers charged with the dangerous task of finding and breaking up illegal stills. Because of its production capacity, even powerful Chicago gangster Al Capone had a hand at one point in the Berkeley County liquor business. Local bootlegger Glennie McKnight expanded his business and became supplier, marketer and distributor for other still operators, helping everyone prosper. As one part of his operation, he reportedly served as a go-between, buying liquor from area distillers and shipping it to Al Capone's gang in Chicago.

Al Capone was photographed at the Chicago detective bureau in 1930, held on a charge of vagrancy. *Courtesy of Chicago Bureau of the FBI via Wikimedia Commons.*

According to Suzannah Smith Miles in the *Charleston Magazine*, Al Capone learned that even a gangland boss couldn't strong-arm the bootleggers in Hell Hole. Reportedly, Capone once failed to pay for a shipment, so Glennie McKnight refused to send any more liquor up north. Six Cadillacs full of henchmen drove to South Carolina to rectify the situation. Glennie's associates stranded the fancy suits deep in the swamp, taking their money and their cars. (If it's not a true story, it should be.)

In 1926, the rivalry between "King of the Bootleggers" Glennie McKnight and his chief local competitor Ben Villeponteaux got bloody. Villeponteaux also had his share of local lawmen and still owners on his side. On May 8, on a road near Moncks Corner, the two groups shot it out. Glennie's brother and a friend died. Villeponteaux and two of his men were wounded. Days later, another man was killed, and his father—known as the "king of Hell Hole Swamp"—was wounded near Huger.

As the violence made national news, Glennie McKnight went rogue. Or did he act as a snitch to avoid a federal indictment? Or was he aiding the feds to get rid of his competition? Rumors were rife. Whatever the reason, Glennie helped the revenuers mount a massive raid on Hell Hole Swamp operators. On September 3, 1926, a small ship brought one hundred deputies into Charleston Harbor. In a two-day assault, seventeen stills were chopped up, thousands of gallons of liquor were poured out and over thirty men were arrested. Large moonshine operations couldn't exist without the protection of law enforcement, who naturally wanted a cut of the lucrative illegal proceeds—but it was still a surprise when the raids also netted the Williamsburg County sheriff and a federal Prohibition agent. Of course, the raid only slowed the production of moonshine in Hell Hole Swamp; it certainly didn't stop it, as the U.S. Senate noted in a later investigation into the Hell Hole Swamp operations.

In 1929, South Carolina's Governor John G. Richards, a fire-breathing prohibitionist, vowed to end the blight and corruption surrounding the illegal liquor business. But the tendrils of illegal activity ran deep and thick into the swamplands, and the political maneuverings got vicious. The governor ordered the county sheriff to fire a deputy working with the moonshiners. The sheriff refused, and the governor—after the state supreme court agreed he had the power—removed the sheriff from office. Then two informants pointed the finger at Berkeley County lawyer and state senator Edward J. Dennis, who they said consorted with the Villeponteaux crowd. Senator Dennis, they claimed, got rich defending bootleggers—or arranging to have their charges dropped—after he got a cut when their liquor was seized by state constables and sold to rival bootleggers. A high-profile trial in Charleston pitted the state senator against a string of bootleggers who testified that he was involved in the rackets. At trial, the jury acquitted Senator Dennis.

Months later, on July 24, 1930, the senator was walking to his law office in Moncks Corner when town character W.L. "Sporty" Thornley balanced the barrel of a shotgun on his car's radiator, took aim and killed the lawyer. Sporty was not bright, a "tubercular, disabled" veteran who said Glennie McKnight offered him money, a house for his family and protection from the police. Sporty received a life sentence for the murder. The senator's son, Rembert Dennis, was appointed to assume his seat, was repeatedly reelected and became one of the state's most influential politicians. And Glennie McKnight and others kept cooking and selling moonshine.

When Prohibition ended in 1933 and liquor could be legally obtained, bootlegging became less lucrative and less popular. Some continued the generations-old traditions, though. Popcorn Sutton, legendary western North Carolina moonshiner, told his story in interviews, in documentaries and in his book *Me and My Likker*, all firsthand accounts that moonshining was a hard way of life. Some bootleggers maintained a high standard for their craft, said Popcorn, while others took deadly, dangerous shortcuts. According to the *Charleston Post and Courier*, "In the 1970s, moonshine coming out of Moncks Corner was the most poisonous in the state due to toxic amounts of lead."

Starting in 1972, celebrants began gathering on the first May weekend around Jamestown's old railroad depot to celebrate the Hell Hole Swamp

The traditional location for the annual Hell Hole Swamp Festival in Jamestown, South Carolina. *Courtesy of Ammondramus via Wikimedia Commons.*

Festival, complete with its "mascot" moonshine still, festival food tents, a parade and the crowning of Miss Hell Hole Swamp.

Anthropologist Dr. Katherine Parker, who studied at the University of South Carolina and earned her doctorate from the renowned anthropology department at the University of Tennessee, began studying moonshining areas in Hell Hole Swamp in the Francis Marion National Forest. Her website showed how old liquor stills look like a trash dump to the untrained eye. She detailed what she looks for in identifying likely sites for excavation: the metal fire box used to heat the still; rocks, bricks or cement blocks to raise the equipment off the ground; glass or stoneware; sheet metal pieces; steel drums; buckets; barrels or barrel rings; and unfired ammunition or casings.

In 2009, South Carolina state law legalized micro-distilleries, and moonshine is now advertised on interstate highway billboards and openly sold, some marketed in screw-top mason jars as a throwback to the old days. Today's legal moonshine ain't your granddaddy's 'shine, though—it's not distilled into a barrel or cooked in a sheltered cove in the woods or deep in the swamp, and there's no need to filter the dead critters and leaves out of the mash. Given that making moonshine is as much culture and tradition as it is alcohol content, the swamp likely continues to hide some stills, and the descendant of some expert distiller in possession of the family recipe is still hauling in fifty-pound sacks of sugar, probably on a four-wheeler.

MURDER SOLVED ON A GRAVESTONE

For all its old-world charm, quaint architecture and shaded, historic walks, Charleston's history had periods that weren't refined and respectable. In the late 1700s, trade routes and rivers from the interior of the state brought animal pelts and farm goods to the thriving port in Charleston to be sold and shipped elsewhere. Those who lived and worked in Charleston or traveled into the city to do business would also need somewhere to slake their thirst or get a filling meal. Taverns abounded, as did thieves, highway robbers and n'er-do-wells.

One tavern stood at the Meeting Street cattle gate near what is now the campus of the College of Charleston. Outside the gate stretched pastures, slaughterhouses and shantytowns—Charleston's early suburbs. The tavern had recently attracted the custom of a group of thieves and ruffians who'd been rousted from another dive near the Ashley River. According to Samuel Stoney's account in Beatrice St. Julien Ravenel's 1947 *Charleston Murders*, a member of the gang stole a lovely bay horse belonging to General Charles Cotesworth Pinckney, a signer of the newly forged U.S. Constitution. In short, Jones Tavern was considered unsavory.

On the evening of March 12, 1788, Nicholas John Wightman, one of four brothers descended from two old Charleston families, left the house he shared with a brother near their silversmith shop to visit one of the reputable taverns near the cattle gate—but just down the street from Jones Tavern. When Nicholas's brother and some friends came looking for him, Nicholas told them to head on back to their shop, farther south on Meeting Street where it intersects Broad Street. He would finish up at the tavern and meet them at the shop. But he never arrived.

His friends walked back up Meeting Street searching for Nicholas and stumbled over his body, slumped in his own blood near the cattle gate, dead. He'd been shot, and a pistol lay nearby.

Then as now, knowing which tavern to frequent and which to avoid in a neighborhood is handy local knowledge. A ruckus at Jones's cattle gate tavern earlier that evening had brought police. A sea captain claimed someone had stolen some Dutch coins from him. Reports said the police were reluctant to enter the tavern—a known hangout for ruffians—until Nicholas's relatives and friends fortuitously showed up after finding him murdered.

The bloody spot where Nicholas's body had fallen attracted a number of sightseers—a precursor to modern-day crime tourists. A boy, identified as the son of a merchant named Edgar Wells, was sharp-eyed enough to pick up a large button embedded in the dusty road. That button, from the cloak of one of the patrons at Jones Tavern, along with the quick work of Nicholas's friends and kin, led to the arrest of the gang responsible for terrorizing the area with robberies, assaults and arson—a serious offense in an era with wooden houses built close together.

General Pinckney, whose stolen horse had been returned, acted as kind and learned counsel to the six defendants. One accused woman was dismissed or acquitted. But the rest were convicted on a variety of charges. Robert Stacy, one of the leaders of the gang and the now-convicted shooter and robber, attempted to refute the evidence from the young son of Edgar Wells and the button he found. Stacy displayed his coat with all the buttons as they should be. But the evidence of the gang's string of crimes, the fear and frustration of the community and perhaps ire at the defendants' prior attacks on everyone who was involved in the prosecution didn't encourage mercy. On June 4, 1788, only weeks after Nicholas Wightman's murder, the hanging of five men and one woman was reported in newspapers as far away as Pennsylvania and Vermont.

Nicholas's brother and sister commissioned engraved stones for his grave that told the story of his death, the solution to his murder and how much his family missed him. The stones lie flat on the ground, just to the right of the gates to the western cemetery of St. Philip's. Across Church Street from St. Philip's massive front doors, the two stones—a triangle and a square—can be seen through the fence railings, though often obscured by shrubbery and encroaching grass. Nicholas's grave marker is badly weathered and unreadable now, but the engraving told the story of a murder and its solution:

> *To the Memory of*
> *Nicholas John Wightman*
> *Who was killed by a Footpad*
> *on the Night of the 12th of March, 1788.*
> *Aged 25 years.*
> *Peaceably returning home*

The gravestones of Nicholas Wightman tell the story of a murder mystery solved. *Photo by Cathy Pickens.*

to his Brother's house
where he resided,
The Villain met and made an attempt
to rob him, which he resisted
and was instantly shot dead on the spot.

The description is continued on the square stone:

His Brother, with but small assistance
the same night, secured the murderer
and six accomplices, being the whole of a gang
that then very much infested the peace of the City,
and by their frequent Robberies,
and attempts to set fire to houses,
kept the inhabitants in constant alarm.
They were shortly tried, and upon the fullest conviction,
Condemned and Executed.
Divine Providence ordered it so that a single button,

Gravestones in Charleston's historic St. Philip's churchyard. *Courtesy of Jim Sill via Flickr.com.*

belonging to the coat of the murderer,
found on the spot where the murder was committed,
by a child, a son of Mr. Edgar Wells, Mercht.,
served, with other proofs, to discover and convict him.
This Marble is erected, by an affectionate Brother & Sister,
in memory of the virtues of their dear Brother,
who was beloved by all who knew him.
He was mild and affable in his manners,
Just, Generous, and Humane.
He is loved with the sincerest affection.
His soul rests at the Mercy Seat of his Creator.

First Lady Eleanor Roosevelt recorded the tombstone's inscription in her syndicated "My Day" newspaper column, which took the place of a personal diary for her. She wrote, "I think in all probability this was the first or one of the first detective stories ever written in this country."

REFERENCES

Welcome

Nuttli, Otto W., G.A. Bollinger and Robert B. Herrmann. "The 1886 Charleston, South Carolina, Earthquake—A 1986 Perspective." U.S. Geological Survey Circular 985. https://pubs.usgs.gov/circ/1986/0985/report.pdf.

1. The Poisoners

The Black Widow

Ford, Wayne. "Mrs. Conyers Enters Guilty Plea to Charge." *Florence Morning News*, May 31, 1977, 2.

Gatling, Holly. "Expert Testifies on Poisoning." *Florence Morning News*, October 2, 1975, 2.

———. "Jury Says Mrs. Conyers Guilty." *Florence Morning News*, October 4, 1975, 1.

High Point Enterprise. "Mrs. Conyers' Trial Continues." September 30, 1975, 2.

State v. Conyers, 233 S.E.2d 95 (1977).

Poison and Punitive Damages

Genay v. Norris, 1 SCL 6, 1 Bay 6 (1784).
Harkup, Kathryn. "Tainted Love: The Poisoner Who Confused Chemicals for Romance." *The Guardian*, February 12, 2016. https://www.theguardian.com.
Trestrail, John Harris III. *Criminal Poisoning*. Humana Press, 2000.

The Poison Cure

Butler, Nic. "Doctor Caesar and His Antidote for Poison in 1750." *Charleston Time Machine*, Charleston County Public Library, February 12, 2021. https://www.ccpl.org.
Gherini, Claire. "Adjudicating 'Caesar's Cure for Poison.'" Hypotheses: The Recipe Project, August 20, 2015. https://recipes.hypotheses.org/6460.

2. LOVE GONE WRONG

Where There's a Will...or a Life Insurance Policy

Rogers, Jamie. "Hanna Gets 440 Years." *Morning News* (Florence, SC), June 1, 2007, 1A.
U.S. v. Hanna, unpublished opinion, US Court of Appeals, 4th Cir., No. 07-4629, December 2, 2009.
U.S. v. Hanna, 4:06-cr-00828-TLW (D.S.C. Apr. 8, 2022).
Wilmington StarNews. "Acquitted of murder, man guilty of fraud." February 24, 2007. https://www.starnewsonline.com.

Deadly Charleston Love Triangle

Leland, Jack. *60 Famous Houses of Charleston*. News & Courier and Evening Post, 1982.
Peck, Thomas K. "The Killing of Captain Dawson," in *Charleston Murders*, edited by Beatrice St. Julian Ravenel. Duell, Sloan and Pierce, 1947.
Williams, Susan Millar, and Stephen G. Hoffius. *Upheaval in Charleston: Earthquake and Murder on the Eve of Jim Crow*. University of Georgia Press, 2011.

3. Serial and Spree Killers

The Folly Beach Killer

Fisher, Joseph C. *Killer Among Us: Public Reactions to Serial Murder*. Praeger, 1997.

Jones, Mark. "Richard Valenti: Super Christian—Serial Killer." Mark Jones Books, February 23, 2016. https://mark-jones-books.com.

Rajaee, Mason J. "Guilty, But Mentally Ill, But Not Insane? Making Sense of South Carolina's Approach to Mentally Ill Offenders." *South Carolina Law Review* 74, no. 3 (August 2023).

State v. Valenti, 218 S.E.2d 726 (1975).

Yee, Gregory. "Folly Beach Killer Richard Valenti Dies in Hospital After Long Illness." *Post and Courier*, December 17, 2020, 3A.

Starting Over

Benson, Michael. *Watch Mommy Die: A Psycho Killer's Vicious Attack*. Kensington Books, 2011.

CBS News. "Murder on His Mind." *48 Hours*, Season 9, Episode 9. First aired January 13, 2007. https://www.cbsnews.com.

Crews, Angela D., PhD, and Gordan A. Crews, PhD. "Living and Dying on Death Row in America." Presented to 16th World Congress: International Society for Criminology, Kobe, Japan, 2011. https://scholarworks.utrgv.edu.

FBI Behavioral Unit. "Serial Murder: Multi-Disciplinary Perspectives for Investigators." Symposium, San Antonio, TX, August 29–September 2, 2005. https://www.fbi.gov.

Garrison, Steve. "South Carolina Inmate Says 'Psychopath' Defense Doomed Him to Death Row." *Courthouse News Service*, March 19, 2024. https://www.courthousenews.com.

Stanko, Stephen, Wayne Gillespie and Gordon A. Crews. *Living in Prison: A History of the Correctional System with an Insider's View*. Greenwood Press, 2004.

Stanko v. Stirling, U.S. Court of Appeals for the Fourth Circuit, July 29, 2024. https://www.ca4.uscourts.gov.

State v. Stanko, 741 S.E.2d 708 (2013).

4. Girls Just Want to Have Fun

Renee Poole

Hardee, J.L. *Justice or Injustice: What Really Happens in a Jury Room*. N.p., 2011.
Hudson, Dale. *Dance of Death*. Pinnacle Books, 2006.
Poole v. Warden of Leath Correctional Institution, Unpublished Opinion of U.S. District Court, Rock Hill Division, January 31, 2007. https://scholar.google.com.
Ropp, Kathy. "Eighteen Years Later, Former Exotic Dancer Convicted of Murder Is Still Fighting to Be Released from Jail." *My Horry News*, May 25, 2018. https://www.myhorrynews.com.
State v. Frazier, 592 S.E.2d 621 (2004).
State v. Frazier, 654 S.E.2d 280 (S.C. App. 2007).
State v. Frazier, 689 S.E.2d 610 (2010).
Website for Free Kimberly Renee Poole: https://www.freekimberly.com.

5. Crime Firsts

The First DNA Case

Hudson, Dale, and Billy Hills. *An Hour to Kill: A True Story of Love, Murder, and Justice in a Small Southern Town*. McGregor Publishing, 1999.
Listrom, Ashley. "Three Decades Later, Family Fights to Keep Loved One's Killer Behind Bars." *WMBF News*, February 14, 2024. https://www.wmbfnews.com.
State v. Register, 419 S.E.2d 771 (1992).
State v. Register, 476 S.E.2d 153 (1995).

The First Female Serial Killer?

Orr, Bruce. *Six Miles to Charleston: The True Story of John and Lavinia Fisher*. The History Press, 2010.
Ravenel, Beatrice St. Julien. "Lovely Lavinia and the Drunken Hangman—1819." In *Charleston Murders*, edited by Beatrice St. Julien Ravenel. Duell, Sloan and Pierce, 1947.

Scott, David C. *Abode of Misery: An Illustrated Compilation of Facts, Secrets and Myths of the Old Charleston District Jail*. Building Art Press, 2010.
Williams, Jack Kenny. *Vogues in Villainy: Crime and Retribution in Antebellum South Carolina*. University of South Carolina Press, 1959.

6. The Unknown

Missing and Not Found

Columbia Record. "Myrtle Beach Man Faces Trial in Vereen Death." March 5, 1986, 38.
Florence Morning News. "Jury Convicts Myrtle Beach Man of Kidnap." January 18, 1985, 15.
Hill, David. "Owens Is Convicted of Murder." *Sun-News* (Myrtle Beach, SC), May 18, 1986, 1.
Larsen, Paul. "Florence Attorney Talks About Trial Experience." *Florence Morning News*, August 21, 1988, 11.
Norton, John. "The Disappearance of Ernie Vereen." *The State*, November 18, 1984, 1.
Shannon, Lesia J. "Journey to Death Row Disturbing." *Sun-News* (Myrtle Beach), November 26, 1990, 1.
———. "State to Seek Death in Owens Retrial." *Sun-News* (Myrtle Beach, SC), November 26, 1990, 1, 5.
State v. Owens, 352 S.E.2d 474 (1986).
State v. Owens, 359 S.E.2d 275 (1987).
State v. Owens, 424 S.E. 2d 473 (1992).
Vereen, Ernest L. The Charley Project, updated December 13, 2018. https://charleyproject.org.
White, Coyte. "Ransom Note Revealed in Kidnapping Trial." *Sun-News* (Myrtle Beach, SC), January 16, 1985, 1.

Oldest Unsolved Murder?

Novelly, Thomas. "A 100-Year-Old Slaying Remains a Mystery in South Carolina." *Post & Courier* (Charleston), January 27, 2020. https://www.courthousenews.com.

Rice, James Henry Jr. "Editorial: The Poor Man and the Game." *The State*, December 30, 1908, 10.
The State. "Pressley Reeves Is Assassinated." September 23, 1908, 1.
Times and Democrat (Orangeburg, SC). "Who Killed Reeves; Testimony Taken at the Coroner's Inquest." December 11, 1908, 9.

A Still Unsolved Case

Beaufort County Sheriff's Office, Cold Case Investigations. March 25, 2021. https://bcso.net/michael-steven-akey/.
Beaufort Gazette. "Fund Drive Initiated for Missing Youth." September 14, 1972, 12.
Yount, Lori. "Body Exhumed for Testing in Revisit of 27-Year-Old Missing Person Case." *Beaufort Gazette*, August 25, 2005, 7.
———. "DNA Test Identifies Remains in 30-Year-Old Case." *Beaufort Gazette*, February 3, 2006, 2.

A Con Man or a Companion?

Berry College. Ellen McClung Berry. Biography prepared for Berry Family Reunion at Berry College, April 18–21, 2013. https://libguides.berry.edu.
Moore, Damion. "The Legend of Dan Tondevold, Part 1." *American Crime Journal*, September 27, 2018. https://americancrimejournal.com/.
———. "The Redemption of Dan Tondevold, Part 2." *American Crime Journal*, November 3, 2018. https://americancrimejournal.com.
Stiles, John H. "Man Wanted in Fraud Case of Gen. White's Kin Shot to Death." *Knoxville News-Sentinel*, April 30, 1985, 1.

7. Family Connections

The Bigham Family

Boling, Katharine. *A Piece of the Fox's Hide*. Ballantine, 1972.
Bovsun, Mara. "Justice Story: The Two Trials of Edmund Bigham." *New York Daily News*, November 11, 2018. https://www.nydailynews.com.

County Record (Kingstree, SC). "Bigham Guilty; Sentenced to Die, Sensational Case Closed." March 31, 1921.

———. "Mrs. E.D. Bigham Released from Jail: Arrested Friday for Trying to Slip Poison to Husband in Prison." March 17, 1921.

Fallon, Eugene. "Ordeal of Edmund Bigham: 'If I Were Guilty of What They Say, I Would Not Want To Live!'" *Rocky Mount Telegram*, Part 2, July 1, 1962, 3B.

———. "Was It the Greatest Outrage Ever Committed in the Carolinas?" *Rocky Mount Telegram*, June 24, 1962, 3B.

State v. Bigham, 112 S.E. 332 (1922).

State v. Bigham, 117 S.E. 57 (1923).

Ziegler, J.A. *The Last of the Bighams*. Sandlapper Publishing, 1984. (Originally published in 1927, copyrighted in 1925.)

Fate and Family

Beaufort Gazette. "Stabs Husband, Commits Suicide: Mrs. Claude Baker Dead After Attacking Husband—Found in Her Home." January 3, 1934, 1.

Monk, John. "Rich Wife Could Be Tried This Year in Arsenic Death." *The State*, February 13, 2005.

Ryan, Jason. *Jackpot: High Times, High Seas, and the Sting That Launched the War on Drugs*. Lyons Press, 2011.

———. *Swamp Kings: The Story of the Murdaugh Family of South Carolina and a Century of Backwoods Power.* Pegasus Crime, 2024.

The State. "Court Convenes at Walterboro." September 22, 1936, 10.

8. THE LAW

McTeer, the High Sheriff

Adams, Samuel Hopkins. "Dr. Bug, Dr. Buzzard and the U.S.A." *True Magazine*, July 1949.

Baxandall, Lee. "Baring Witness: America's First Nudist Colony Had a South Carolina Address." South Carolina Progressive Network, September 12, 1995. https://www.scpronet.com.

McTeer, J.E., with Kent W. Nickerson, editor. *High Sheriff of the Low Country*. Beaufort Book Co., 1970.

Woods, Baynard. *Coffin Point: The Strange Cases of Ed McTeer, Witchdoctor Sheriff*. River City Publishing, 2010.

Melvin Purvis

Ford, Bob. "Purvis, Melvin Horace, Jr." *South Carolina Encyclopedia*, June 20, 2016, updated August 22, 2022. https://www.scencyclopedia.org.

Lathan, S. Robert.M.D. "Experience of My Famous Uncle, Melvin Purvis, with Hoover's Jealousy and with Nazi Hermann Göring." *Proceedings Baylor University Medical Center* 29, no. 3 (July 2016): 348–51. https://www.ncbi.nlm.nih.gov.

Purvis, Alston, and Alex Tresniowski. *The Vendetta: FBI Hero Melvin Purvis's War Against Crime, and J. Edgar Hoover's War Against Him*. Public Affairs, 2005.

Reuben Greenberg

Greenberg, Reuben, with Arthur Gordon. *Let's Take Back Our Streets!* Contemporary Books, 1989.

MacDougall, David W. "ATM Installed in Police Lobby." *Post and Courier* (Charleston, SC), December 17, 1994, 1.

Morrill, Jim. "Police Chief Takes Common-Sense Approach." *Charlotte Observer*, January 22, 1994, 1C.

Post and Courier. "Where's Reuben? Former Charleston Police Chief Opens Up About His Retirement in North Carolina Mountains, Health Issues That Led to His Departure." April 13, 2008.

Rosen Hagood Law Firm. "Remembering the Contributions of Police Chief Reuben Greenberg." February 25, 2021. https://rosenhagood.com.

Siegel, Barry. "Black Police Chief Skates Past Skeptics." *Los Angeles Times*, October 3, 1983, 1.

9. Side Trips, Crime Bits and Oddities

The Lizard Man of Scape Ore Swamp

Blackburn, Lyle. *Lizard Man: The True Story of the Bishopville Monster*. Anomalist Books, 2013.

ETV Road Show. "Lizard Man of Lee County." YouTube, https://www.youtube.com.

Georgas, George. "Bumps in the Night? Lee County Seeks 'Lizard' with Bad Attitude." *The Item* (Sumter, SC), July 20, 1988, 1.

Lutz, Alicia. "Professors Search for Lizard Man in S.C." *The College Today* (College of Charleston), July 3, 2015. https://today.cofc.edu.

Poole, W. Scott. *Monsters in America: Our Historical Obsessions with the Hideous and the Haunting*. Baylor University Press, 2011.

South Carolina Public Radio. "30 Years Later, the Legend of the Lizard Man Lives on in Bishopville." June 15, 2018. https://www.southcarolinapublicradio.org.

Moonshine and Hell Hole Swamp

Hutcheson, Neal. *The Moonshiner Popcorn Sutton*. N.p., 2021.

Lewis, S. Duane, and Daniel J. Crooks. *Lawmen and Lawlessness: Historic Cases of Corruption and Murder Investigated by the Sheriffs of Berkeley County, S.C. 1882 to 1970*. Palmetto Publishing, 2022.

Miles, Suzannah Smith. "Moonshine Over Hell Hole Swamp." *Charleston Magazine*, December 2015. https://charlestonmag.com.

Parker, Katherine G. "Francis Marion National Forest (FMNF) Still Sites." https://www.katherineparkerarchaeology.com.

Smith, Fleming. "SC's Moonshine Culture and Its Long, Bullet-Riddled History." *Post and Courier*, January 10, 2020; updated January 21, 2021. https://www.postandcourier.com.

Video links to Popcorn Sutton documentary "This Is the Last Dam Run of Likker I'll Ever Make." https://www.youtube.com/watch?v=glQjCKAI4gA, and interviews with SuckerPunchPictures [https://www.youtube.com/@SuckerPunchPictures]. Also available on DVDs.

Murder Solved on a Gravestone

Independent Gazetteer (Philadelphia, PA). "Charleston, March 15." March 28, 1788, 2.

King, William L. *The Newspaper Press of Charleston, S.C.: A Chronological and Biographical History, Embracing a Period of One Hundred and Forty Years.* Edward Perry (Book Press), 1872.

Roosevelt, Eleanor. "My Day—April 30, 1937." https://www2.gwu.edu.

Stoney, Samuel Gaillard. "The Footpad's Memorial—1788." In *Charleston Murders*, edited by Beatrice St. Julien Ravenel. Duell, Sloan & Pierce, 1947.

ABOUT THE AUTHOR

Cathy Pickens, a lawyer and college professor, is a crime fiction writer (*Southern Fried Mysteries*, St. Martin's/Minotaur and Joffe Books) and true crime columnist for *Mystery Readers Journal*. She is a professor emerita in the McColl School of Business and has served as national president of Sisters in Crime and on the boards of Mystery Writers of America and the Mecklenburg Forensic Medicine Program (an evidence collection/preservation training collaborative). She is also the author of *CREATE!* (ICSC Press), offers coaching and workshops on developing the creative process and works with writers on telling their stories.

Other History Press books by the author:

Charlotte True Crime Stories
True Crime Stories of Eastern North Carolina
Triangle True Crime Stories
True Crime Stories of the Triad
True Crime Stories of Upstate South Carolina
True Crime Stories of Western North Carolina
True Crime Stories of South Carolina's Midlands
Charleston Mysteries